GW00467530

DON'T HAVE
NIGHTMARES !

TRUE GHOSTS AND GHOULS OF WINDSOR & ETON

BRIAN LANGSTON

HALSGROVE

First published in Great Britain in 2016

British Library Cataloguing-in-Publication Data
A CIP record for this title is available from the British Library

ISBN 978 0 85704 289 7

HALSGROVE
Halsgrove House,
Ryelands Industrial Estate,
Bagley Road, Wellington, Somerset TA21 9PZ
Tel: 01823 653777   Fax: 01823 216796
email: sales@halsgrove.com

Part of the Halsgrove group of companies
Information on all Halsgrove titles is available at: www.halsgrove.com

Printed and bound in China by Everbest Printing Investment Ltd

For my darling Podley – Peas and Love forever.

CONTENTS

WARNING !

This book contains true accounts of disturbing paranormal
activity which might frighten anyone of a nervous disposition.
If you chose to continue reading, you do so at your own risk.

I hope you enjoy it!

AUTHOR'S FOREWORD

WHEN WILLIAM THE Conqueror decided to built his fortress on the banks of the Thames at Windsor, he couldn't have imagined that his legacy would endure for almost a thousand years and have played such a significant role in the proud story of our nation. Similarly the enormous impact that Windsor's sleepy neighbour, Eton, has had on our history through Henry VI's Eton College, over the past six centuries, is nothing short of incredible.

This quiet picturesque little corner of Berkshire out-punches its weight on all fronts, including the incidence of paranormal phenomena. For some unknown reason, the geographically tiny area of Windsor and Eton has a highly-charged supernatural DNA, perhaps as a consequence of the enormous levels of emotional energy which have been absorbed by its ancient streets over centuries of turmoil and turbulence. If England is the most haunted country in the world then Windsor's Royal Borough must surely qualify as one of the most haunted and mysterious places on earth.

I have always been fascinated by mysteries and the unexplained and this is one of the reasons why I joined the police. During a long and eventful career, most of which was spent in Berkshire, I had the misfortune to meet many monsters, but none of them were paranormal. All were very much flesh and blood including the Yorkshire Ripper, Peter Sutcliffe, who I interviewed in Broadmoor along with the psychopathic crime baron Ronnie Kray. There are some cases of real-life ghouls in this book but for the most part its focus is on the many supernatural entities who stalk the historic streets of Windsor and Eton.

Detectives are taught Locard's Law; that every contact leaves a trace. More often than not this does not apply to the supernatural world where physical evidence is not always apparent. But even where tangible proof is absent, there can be no doubt of the enormous emotional impact which many witnesses report after a paranormal encounter.

As well as celebrating the rich occult heritage of the area and the celebrated Royal phantoms of Windsor Castle, this book chronicles the experiences of many ordinary people who have experienced mystifying events in their own homes and workplaces which defy rational explanation. Some of their stories are amongst the most persuasive and petrifying and are related here in print for the first time.

It is often said that truth is scarier than fiction and I trust that the following stories will reinforce this, as you embark upon a journey through the dark and often macabre history of the *True Ghosts and Ghouls of Windsor & Eton.*

Brian Langston
March 2016
email: ghostsofwindsor@gmail.com
www.brianlangston.com
@ghostsofwindsor

ACKNOWLEDGEMENTS

MY SINCERE THANKS to everyone who has contributed to this book, most of whom have done so on the proviso that I do not reveal their true identity. This helpfully eliminates the need for me to thank you by name – but you know who you are and your help has been greatly appreciated.

People have been only too willing to share their personal experiences of unusual and supernatural happenings and I have been touched by the kindness of friends and strangers who have helped me in my research by running errands, visiting libraries and providing me with stories and supporting information.

A special thanks to the Forumites of the Royal Windsor Website for being so generous in sharing their extensive knowledge of their historic home town – not to mention their photos. Thanks too to members of the Berkshire Paranormal Group who have so helpfully contributed to the writing of this book by sharing the results of some of their nocturnal investigations, many of which from the surrounding villages, will have to be carried over to a future book.

A particular thank you to my wife Jenny who has spent many long hours researching and unearthing stories with unstinting efficiency, so that no sooner had I declared the book finished, that she came up with another half dozen tales which she had resurrected from the mists of time. Her patience in wading through drafts of the manuscript has been above and beyond the call of duty.

PART ONE
WINDSOR CASTLE

··

Chapter 1
WINDSOR'S TORMENTED TOWERS

IT IS DIFFICULT to imagine a more appropriate place to find a ghost than Windsor Castle. It has been the residence of every English monarch since the Norman Conquest and has endured over nine hundred years of splendour, blood, crime, romance, tragedy and suffering.

The tormented towers have seen a grim tally of distinguished prisoners across the centuries.

1265 - The Lord Mayor FitzThomas was imprisoned here and never seen again.

1346 - King John II of France and King David II of Scotland were imprisoned in the comparative luxury of the Upper Ward here until their ransom was paid.

1413 - The Earl of March and Prince James (later James I) of Scotland were imprisoned here.

1546 - The poet, the Earl of Surrey, was imprisoned at Windsor Castle

1647 - King Charles I was imprisoned at Windsor Castle before being transferred to Carisbrooke Castle on the Isle of Wight.

The Round Tower
The ghost of William Wykeham former Lord Chancellor to Edward III and Bishop of Winchester is one of the earliest ghosts known to haunt the Castle and has done so since his death in 1404. As the architect of much of the Castle in the fourteenth century, his presence is a benign one and his smiling countenance has been seen standing on the top of the Round Tower proudly surveying his work. His motto was *'Manners makyth man'*. It is not surprising therefore that those who have seen him have described the experience as 'tranquil and peaceful'.

Mrs Mary Parsons, the wife of England's oldest soldier had a ghostly experience when she lived in the Round Tower with her husband Gunner Samuel Parsons. Gunner Parsons joined the army in 1844 and saw action at the battles of Inkerman and Balaclava during the Crimean War. In 1859 he was posted to Windsor Castle with the responsibility for raising and lowering the Union flag and Royal Standard on the top of the Round Tower at sunrise and sunset. Remarkably over half a century later in 1912, he was still in the same post as a serving soldier at the ripe age of eighty-seven years.

The couple experienced many unexplained occurrences during the time they lived in the historic Royal Tower. One night after Mrs Parsons had gone to bed, she heard a great commotion outside her bedroom door. Her husband was asleep beside her and no-one else was in the Tower. As she sat up and watched the door, she saw the door handle turn and an invisible presence pushed the door wide open. She threw her head under the bedclothes in terror and remained there until dawn. She saw or heard nothing more but was unable to explain how the ancient heavy door had opened by itself.

The Curfew Tower
The Curfew Tower built in 1319 contains a belfry which, during the Middle Ages, used to toll nightly to mark the 8pm curfew. Its dominating position above the town made it ideal as the site of public executions. For centuries prisoners dragged from the dungeons below were hanged from a beam at the top of the 100 foot tower, their bodies often remaining there for weeks as a deterrent to the Windsor townsfolk.

The religious turmoil of King Henry VIII's reign impacted heavily on Windsor. In 1536, during the Dissolution of the Monasteries, two Windsor men were hanged for their overly Catholic beliefs. A local priest was accused of supporting the revolutionary *'Pilgrimage of Grace'* and was hanged from a tree near Windsor Bridge. He implicated a local butcher who then suffered the same fate at the Castle Gate, although local tradition suggests that the butcher, Mark Fytton, was actually hanged for selling poisoned meat which caused the death of many local people.

Whatever their crimes, their bodies were then displayed from the gibbet at the top of the Curfew Tower until they rotted. Recently officers from the Royalty Protection Team, responsible for securing the rooftops during State events, confirmed that the hook, from which the corpses were suspended, still exists at the top of the Tower.

However Henry was nothing if not even-handed and just six years later it was the turn of Protestants to be persecuted. Anthony Pearson a popular local preacher, Henry Filmer a churchwarden and Robert Testwood a lay-clerk at St George's Chapel were rounded up for their over-zealous Protestantism, on the strength of evidence from a Catholic former mayor, William Simmonds who had an axe to grind against them. On 4 August 1543, *'The Windsor Martyrs'*, as they were later to be known, were publicly burnt alive in a field within sight of the Curfew Tower where the Windsor & Eton Riverside Station now stands. It was said that their screams of agony could be heard for many years afterwards and on certain days can still be heard today.

Given its miserable history both as a dungeon and place of execution, it is scarcely surprising that the Curfew Tower has many ghostly phenomena associated with it. The sounds of phantom footsteps have often been heard on the stone steps leading up to the top of the Tower and on one occasion an observer reported that the temperature suddenly plummeted and the bells began to swing inexplicably of their own accord.

The Devil's Tower

The octagonal Edward III Tower was formerly known as the Devil's Tower or the Maids of Honour Tower as it was used in the eighteenth century by the ladies in attendance on the Royal Family. It was dubbed the Devil's Tower by the medieval masons who believed they were being thwarted by supernatural forces when they tried to first build it. The story is that they tried for six years to raise a parapet but each night the Devil appeared and, brick by brick, took it down again before dawn. Eventually their persistence paid off and the Tower was finished and soon became a favourite place of imprisonment and torture. Many of the tormented souls incarcerated there were never seen alive again.

The Devil's Tower from a sketch by Dr William Crotch 1832.
Creative Commons © Yale Center for British Art, Paul Mellon Collection

King John used the Castle as a prison to incarcerate his political enemies. In 1210 Maud de Braose and her son William were captured in Ireland and brought to Windsor where they were thrown into a dungeon at the Castle and deliberately starved to death. Although some chroniclers suggest this tragic incident may have taken place at Corfe Castle, this wanton act of despicable cruelty further alienated the Barons towards John, and hastened the signing of the Magna Carta five years later.

King Richard III, the ruthless chief suspect in the murder of the Princes in the Tower of London, is also believed to have walled up his enemies in the Towers at Windsor and their bodies have never been found. Over the centuries many have reported the heart-rending and terrifying sight of phantoms emerging from the walls of the Tower ragged, wretched and begging for mercy.

Among the prisoners kept in the Castle in the reign of Henry VI were several people accused of witchcraft and sorcery, the best known of them being Margery Jourdemain, known as 'The Witch of Eye', who was held in Windsor for two years on unspecified charges of sorcery. Margery had for many years been known as someone who could provide spells and potions useful in advancing love and bringing about a pregnancy or ending one. She is immortalised in this early poem;

'There was a Beldame called the wytch of Ey,
Old mother Madge her neyghbours did hir name
Which wrought wonders in countryes by heresaye
Both feendes and fayries her charmyng would obay
And dead corpsis from grave she could uprere
Suche an inchauntresse, as that tyme had no peere.'

She was released from Windsor in 1431 on condition that she refrained from further witchcraft. Regrettably it seems she failed to heed the warning and ten years later she found herself re-arrested by the King's men and taken to the Tower of London. This time she was found guilty of heresy and witchcraft and sentenced to an horrific death by burning at Smithfield.

For centuries the Devil's Tower had a fearsome reputation both as a dreaded place of incarceration but also as being a place haunted by the tormented souls of its former dead. Even as late as 1769 in *Deliciæ Britannicæ; or The Curiosities of Hampton Court and Windsor,* George Bickham writes of the Devil's Tower;

'...The reason why this last Tower has for a long time been so distinguished, was a received notion, as we are informed, that formerly it was haunted by evil spirits.'

Reassuringly he then adds: '...For many years however, it has been inhabited, without the least interruption or disturbance, as far as we can find, from such aerial visitors.'

The Seabrook Tower

A lady visiting Seabrook Tower in 1873 had a bizarre encounter with a group of mysterious figures near St George's Chapel. She wrote a detailed description of the incident at the time;

> 'One evening in 1873 I was visiting some friends who then resided in the Seabrook Tower of Windsor Castle. It was a calm night and there was no moon. I passed down the broad roadway leading to Castle Hill. My attention was arrested where now is the site of St George's Chapel, by a magnificent group of statuary in black. It stood on the left side as I walked down the roadway. The figures presented were three bending and the crouching form of a fourth. The centre figure had in his hand a large sword which was as if in the act of striking. The figures interested me greatly, but I had never seen them before, although I was well acquainted with the Castle.
>
> The thought that occurred to me was that it had not been there that morning and it surely could not have been put up in so few hours. I stood looking at the group for some minutes.
>
> Going out the entrance I spoke to the sentry there, told him what I had seen and asked him if he knew anything about it. He came as far as the end of his beat and said he could go no further, so I went on a few yards before him, in order to point out where I had seen it. When I got to the spot it had gone. I went home and have often wondered what it was I saw, or what it was I was caused to have seen but I have never been able to discover.'

Had she witnessed a medieval re-enactment of a scene of *coup de grâce* or possibly experienced a time slip into an earlier chapter of the Castle's violent history? This fascinating incident remains a mystery.

The Mary Tudor Tower

For many years there have been reports of ghostly footsteps on the stairs in the Mary Tudor Tower in the Lower Ward. During the early part of the twentieth century it was the home of General Sir Charles Kavanagh, the Governor of the Military Knights. His daughter often reported hearing footsteps coming up the steps late at night and stopping outside her bedroom door. Later during her life she discovered that previous occupants of the tower going back decades had reported the same phenomenon.

Her mother Lady Kavanagh was categoric that their home was haunted by a ghost which she described as 'a woman in a grey dress and a white cap' whom she saw several times. Princess Alice (the Countess of Athlone), who was the last surviving grandchild of Queen Victoria, had a keen interest in the supernatural and insisted on having a séance in the drawing room, during which it emerged that the ghost was an Elizabethan serving maid who was badly mistreated when in service and had an illegitimate child whilst living at the

Castle. This had happened in the time of a Governor called De Burgh. Subsequent enquiries verified this story in old Castle archives.

In another bedroom nearby, overnight guests reported that one of the partition walls appeared to move as they lay in bed before going to sleep. Whether this was an optical illusion or a glimpse of an earlier layout remains uncertain.

The Norman Tower

The Norman Tower which adjoins Windsor's famous Round Tower has also been the home of many hauntings over the centuries which continue to this day. The Prison Room, above the Norman Gate was used as a prison during the Civil War and is haunted by the ghost of an elderly man, believed to be a former Royalist prisoner from the Civil War. He has appeared to children playing in the room but has caused them no distress. Many people have experienced the sensation of someone brushing against them or in some cases pushing past them on the stairs and in the old stone passages.

The Garter Tower

The Garter Tower is part of the long, pleasant line of houses in which the Military Knights now live. It lies near the King Henry VIII gateway, through which most people enter the Castle.

An old guidebook to the Castle from the nineteenth century reads;

'Here during the reign of Queen Elizabeth a manservant is said to have killed a maid. Beyond the bare fact of the supposed murder, history provides no information. But believers in ghosts, and, in particular, one official who lived in the Tower for some years, are quite sincere in their declaration that the ghost of the maid walks the house at night.

The very old servants and officials in the Castle do not agree in their belief in ghosts. Some say they have met them, some laugh at the idea but it is interesting to put some of the winding passages and solemn towers to "the old dog" test and see what happens. It is usually believed that dogs sense the supernatural before any human being, and it is also true that, on several occasions, dogs, have nervously refused to enter some of the Castle towers. When one considers the history of the Castle, the stories of such tragedies as the burial alive of his enemies by King John, who walled his victims in and left them to an awful death, it is difficult to believe – if one believes in ghosts at all – that so much could happen without leaving some ghostly echo to remind those of today of the tragedies of yesterday.'

The Saxon Tower

An unnamed but *'well known Windsor man'* who lived near to the Castle was walking close to the Saxon Tower at dusk during the summer of 1926 when he was surprised to see the figure of a woman in medieval dress looking out of one of the windows.

He knew the tower had been uninhabited for many years and, his curiosity aroused, he stood and watched the figure for some minutes. He described her as; *'tall and thin, dressed in black and with her face partly hidden by a sort of cowl or veil.'*

As he watched she vanished suddenly as if she had dropped through the floor. Then to his astonishment the apparition appeared a few minutes later on the battlements and, as he was watching it, it gently faded away.

The description matched those given by a sentry some years previously who whilst standing by his box on the East Terrace caught sight of a hooded woman walking towards him. Before he had time to challenge her, she flung herself kneeling at his feet and then vanished. The soldier was ridiculed when he reported the incident and was accused of falling asleep on duty, but he was adamant about what he had seen. In both cases the phantom figure was attributed to Elizabeth I.

Another ghostly sighting at Christmas 1963 was also believed to be the Virgin Queen. Two Castle guards patrolling the battlements reported seeing the figure of a woman in black with a curious olive complexion appear before them. They saw the wind blowing through her long red hair but as they approached her, she vanished.

King John's Tower

In 1906 when King Edward and Queen Alexandra were at Windsor just before the death of King Christian IX of Denmark, one of the maid servants, who for a number of years had been in the employ of the Queen, became so ill with fright at a hideous apparition she encountered in King John's Tower, that she had to be sent home under medical care.

Exactly what terrifying spectre, the poor maid saw was never disclosed, due to an uncompromising gagging order on the part of King Edward VII. Stories of screaming banshees spread like wildfire through the Royal Household, creating alarm and panic and several members of staff refused to enter certain haunted parts of the Castle. Rumours of a ghost-inspired domestic rebellion reached the ears of the King who was said to be furious. Fearing a mass exodus of servants, Edward issued an edict to silence the *'foolish talk about ghosts'*. He forbade all talk about spectres at Windsor Castle on pain of severe punishment and dismissal. The Queen's maid never recovered from the shock of what she saw in King John's Tower and was never well enough to return to work at the Castle.

King Edward's hard line prevailed for many years and to an extent still survives to this day, accounting for the decline in reported sightings over the past century and the blanket, 'no comment' policy, on all things supernatural from the Royal Household. Indeed in subsequent decades, Royal tour guides were instructed to remove all references to ghosts from their Windsor Castle tours and instead stick strictly to 'historical facts'.

And yet Edward's approach was motivated by simple economic pragmatism (the need to retain 3000 servants and staff who were essential to the running of the Castle) rather than by any disbelief in the supernatural. On the contrary, he himself claimed to have seen the ghost of Elizabeth I, and as a young man walking the dark corridors of the Castle with his younger brother Prince Alfred, the Duke of Edinburgh, they both saw a horrifying spectral figure appear before them. Edward who was carrying a heavy book at the time hurled it at the unidentified phantasm. The book passed through the ghostly figure and knocked off a bust of Sir Robert Peel, sending it crashing to the floor in smithereens. For this, he later admitted, he received a severe rebuke from Queen Victoria for this disgraceful ill-treatment of one of her early Prime Ministers.

Queen Alexandra herself told several people at the Castle that she often heard ghostly music and singing, and that once in her own dressing room she saw a ghost. It is not known whether this was the same spectre which so disturbed her maid, but the following week she invited a famous medium to Windsor and began a long interest in spiritualism. At one séance it is said the medium predicted the early death of King Edward VIII and the outbreak of the Great War.

The Deanery

Throughout the twentieth Century, several people reported seeing a ghostly Canon emerge from the door of St Georges' Chapel and walk a few paces towards the Deanery before disappearing into thin air. His identity remains unknown and this ecclesiastic apparition has not been seen for many years.

The author Hector Bolitho whilst staying at the Deanery in the 1940s reported hearing the sound of footsteps walking outside the corridor of his bedroom. He also heard the distinct change of tone when the footsteps mounted a little flight set of steps and then continued on along the passageway. What bewildered him was that he plainly heard four steps being mounted when he knew full well that there were only three as he had climbed them several times during his stay. He ran to the door and peered out into the corridor but there was no-one in sight.

He later told a member of the Royal Household of his experience and was informed that the floor level had been raised and originally there were indeed four steps but one had been eliminated in building works many years before. The footsteps he heard had been one of the many ghosts whose restless spirits roam the ancient Deanery.

It is not known whether these footsteps belonged to the ghost of a sad little boy who was also seen in the Deanery in the 1930s standing in the doorway of one of the bedrooms of the Canon's house saying *'I don't want to go riding today.'* The startled observer then saw the poignant phantom vanish in front of him.

In late September 1900 rumours began to circulate around Windsor that sentries patrolling the cloisters near the Albert Memorial Chapel at midnight had seen a ghostly figure in white, haunting the ancient dark recesses. This led to speculation that the apparition was the wraith of Prince Albert who had returned to collect Queen Victoria and lead her into the next life. At this time the Queen was eighty-one years old and in very poor health. The gossip was considered to be in very bad taste and was quickly stamped out by Castle officials. Nevertheless Victoria's condition deteriorated and within a few weeks she did indeed join her beloved Albert after a separation of forty years.

The Horseshoe Cloister
At the west end of the Lower Ward lies the distinctively shaped Horseshoe Cloister, originally built in 1480 near to St George's Chapel to house its clergy. This curved brick and timber building is said to have been designed to resemble the shape of a fetlock, one of the badges used by Edward IV.

In recent times the Cloister has been used as accommodation for the Royal Household. A London taxi driver reported that when he was a child he lived in one of the houses in the Horseshoe Cloister. One day whilst washing his hands at the sink in the basement kitchen he heard the sound of hooves on the brick floor. He turned around, startled by the noise, and saw the figure of a man in a leather jerkin leading a horse right through the kitchen which then vanished into a wall opposite. The maid-of-all-work who was present at the time also saw this. Terrified by what they had seen, they reported it to the rest of the family who dismissed it as overactive imagination. Some time later however when repairs were being undertaken in the kitchen, a large underground stable was found behind the wall where the horse and groom had disappeared. This was believed to have been early stable accommodation for cavalry officers stationed within the Castle.

The ghost of a woman in white was reported to appear frequently on the stroke of 6pm. She was seen several times by the Head Chorister of St George's Chapel and his family who lived in another house in the Horseshoe Cloister. Although they were not troubled by this ghostly presence, subsequent tenants were alarmed by an entity which materialised before them, and were promptly re-housed.

The ghost of a child has also been seen elsewhere in the Horseshoe Cloister. A woman living there in the late nineteenth century was surprised to see the odd figure of a young girl dressed in blue standing beside a Christmas tree. When she went over to investigate the curious sight, both the girl and the tree vanished in front of her. The woman fled in terror.

A long-forgotten Castle ghost, not reported for many years, is that of a huge spectral black hound. The origin of this beast is not known. Some have suggested it is one of Herne the Hunter's hell-hounds *(see Chapter 19)*. Others believe it to be the ghost of a bull mastiff kept by one of the medieval Kings. For centuries it haunted the terraces around the Castle and terrified the sentries when it appeared. Charles Knight the famous Windsor publisher and Royal commentator even reported during the clamour of the general election of 1812, that the ghostly black dog of Windsor had appeared on the North Terrace complete with fearfully clanking chains. He recalled that as a child he was aware of the terrible reputation of this dreaded beast.

Windsor Castle's Haunted Portrait

Some parapsychologists believe that the centuries of traumatic events which have taken place at the Castle have left a psychic imprint on the fabric of the building. This is referred to as the 'stone tape' theory and indeed many mysterious occurrences have been reported in the ancient stone rooms. One unusual ghost story is told by members of the Royal Household about a haunted portrait which once hung in Windsor Castle, which allegedly helped to bring a murderer to justice with a message from the grave.

During the latter years of Queen Victoria's reign when the Royal Court had left Windsor for the summer, a young man called Treleven came on a visit to his uncle who was an official at the Castle. The room he had allotted to him was not the grand suite he had been hoping for. It was damp, very small and had an unimpressive view over the rear of the Castle. It was sparsely furnished and had clearly not been used for many years.

The one thing in the room which did attract his attention as soon as he entered, was an oil painting. It was the portrait of a young man not unlike himself, which was hanging over the mantel shelf. The longer he looked at the face in the frame the more it fascinated him, until gradually he found himself being hypnotized by it. He lay on the bed and found himself drifting into a trance-like state. When he awoke a few minutes later he was amazed to find himself out-of-doors. He was in a dark and eerie wooded meadow next to a river and had an overwhelming feeling of fear and foreboding. As he tried to gather his senses he heard two men approaching and, feeling very anxious, hid behind an oak tree and watched.

He saw two men walking side by side and engaged in an animated conversation. The taller of the two wore a tweed suit, and had a sandy beard and whiskers. His eyes were a steely blue and set close together, and Treleven took an instinctive dislike to him. The other man he recognised at once. He was the living embodiment of the young man in the portrait. As the men passed by him, he noticed the young man had very long, white hands, and on one of his fingers was a signet ring with a big stone in it which was clearly visible in the portrait. The two men walked on and were then lost from view amongst the trees and shadows, although Treleven could still hear their voices.

Then all of a sudden he heard the voices grow louder as if they were in a violent argument. He heard the sound of a struggle followed by a splash and a cry which died away in a piteous wail. Then all was silent and the scene began to fade into blackness. At that point Treleven regained consciousness and found himself back on the bed in his dingy Castle room staring up at the portrait.

He assumed he had been dreaming and said nothing to anyone that evening but during the night the experience played on his mind and the following morning he asked his uncle about the history of the portrait. The uncle then told him the tragic story of the young man who, a few years before had gone walking with a relative by the Thames and had tragically fallen in and been drowned despite the best efforts of his relative to rescue him. Treleven told his uncle about his 'vision' and to his amazement accurately described the relative in question.

The story goes that the guilty relative was later confronted and confessed to his crime, begging forgiveness, although as with many such stories, any official confirmation of this is lacking. Whether this is simply an apocryphal tale shared by the servants at the Castle or whether it has any basis in truth is open to question. After this incident it is said that the portrait was removed into storage but the room where it once hung, retains a haunted reputation and is no longer used.

Chapter 2
SCEPTRED SPECTRES

King Henry VIII

THE GHOST OF Henry VIII, probably the most well-known of the Tudor monarchs, has been seen on several occasions roaming the ancient Castle. He is known to haunt the Deanery where his ghost is purported to walk through the cloisters, dragging his ulcerated legs and groaning from the pain.

Henry VIII was born at Greenwich in 1491 and succeeded to the throne after his father's death in 1509. Henry married his brother's widow, Catherine of Aragon but divorced her when she did not produce a male heir to the throne. In 1534, Henry broke away from the Catholic church and proclaimed himself head of the Church of England creating a period of unrivalled religious turbulence known as 'The Dissolution of the Monasteries'.

Henry was an athletic youth and was known to have spent many happy times at Windsor Castle, however it was a near-fatal accident at Greenwich Palace in 1536 which changed his life forever and may have indirectly led to the death of Anne Boleyn. During a tournament, Henry, in full armour was thrown from his heavily armoured horse which then fell on top of him. He was unconscious for over two hours and not expected to survive the fall. A message was sent to Anne Boleyn who was pregnant with their first child, telling her to prepare herself for his death. The shock, she later claimed, caused her to miscarry the baby boy she was carrying. The failure to bear Henry a male heir was to prove fatal for Anne just a few months later.

Although he recovered from the accident, he was plagued with ill health forever afterwards and his leg became chronically ulcerated requiring constant attention for the rest of his life. Recent studies have suggested that Henry also sustained an undiagnosed brain injury during this accident which changed his personality and created the tyrant that he subsequently became. By the time he died in 1547 at the age of fifty-six, his body was riddled with syphilitic sores. It is estimated that he weighed 28 stone, was barely able to walk, had fading eyesight and was plagued with paranoia and melancholy.

It is this fearsome bloated figure that has been seen walking the ancient corridors at Windsor. Several witnesses have described him as *being a large anxious, angry man.* His heavy laboured footsteps have been heard pacing back and forth and at times he is heard shouting.

So regular was his mournful moaning heard, that there was a time when it was ascribed to the sound of the wind coming up The Hundred Steps, but even at night when the door to the steps has been closed, the same eerie noise has been heard.

In 1977 two guards patrolling the battlements saw the unmistakeable apparition of the Tudor King vanishing into the brickwork. Later they were told that a doorway used to exist at the spot where they saw his ghost disappear. More recently a young guardsman fainted after an encounter with the monstrous monarch.

His spirit it seems has not wandered far from his earthly remains which lie in a modest tomb in the Quire of St George's Chapel alongside that of his third wife Jane Seymour, who died in childbirth, bearing him the son and heir he was so desperate for. However, even in death his body was not left to rest in peace.

For many years after the death of his daughter Mary, there were *'whisperings'* that she had dug up and burnt his bones. *'Bloody'* Mary had caused so much suffering during her fanatical reign to restore Catholicism, that many readily believed the myth that she had watched her father's bones burn whilst chanting; *'Tonight father we are truly burning a heretic.'*

This was proven to be a complete falsehood when the tomb was opened in 1649 to receive the body of Charles I. The Royal cadaver was found to be intact and complete- although not for long. In a fascinating memoir kept hidden for decades by the faithful retainer to King Charles, Sir Thomas Herbert described the desecration of Henry's tomb by an intruder. When the Chapel was cleared for the secret burial of the beheaded monarch in the vault, keys were handed to the Sexton who secured the chapel while whilst the workmen prepared to seal the coffin. However a foot soldier had secreted himself in a dark corner of the Chapel and took the opportunity to plunder Henry's tomb. He cut off a section of the velvet pall which covered the top and smashed a hole through the lead casing and reached in

Engraving of Henry VIII by Wenceslas Hollar.
Wikimedia Commons

through the side of the wooden coffin within. Searching inside for anything of value he pulled out an object which turned out to be one of the King's metacarpal bones from his hand, which he wrapped in the velvet and hid in his clothing. Whilst trying to make his escape, he was caught by the Sexton and the alarm was raised. The soldier was searched and the bone discovered on his person. He admitted he was going to use it as the handle for a knife. The Royal relic was returned to the tomb and the guard was *'severely dealt with'* by the Governor of the Castle, although his exact fate is not recorded.

This was not the first time that Henry's body had been dishonoured after his death. During the break with Rome, there was public outcry at his relationship with the loathed Anne Boleyn, who was considered by many to be a witch.

In a remarkably brave gesture a Franciscan friar, Father Peto, in a prophetic sermon, compared Henry and Anne Boleyn to the biblical King Ahab and his wife Jezebel who replaced the true prophets with pagan priests. This was a clear reference to Henry's systematic eradication of Catholicism in favour of Lutheranism. Father Peto went on to warn Henry that if he continued to behave in this way his corpse would suffer the same indignity that had befallen the Israelite King, namely that after his death wild dogs would lick his blood.

Although furious at the sermon, which was widely applauded by the common people, Henry had not yet reached his tyrannical heights and surprisingly the friar managed to keep his head.

After his death in 1547, Henry's body lay in state for over two weeks but there was no great outpouring of grief. On St Valentine's Day his body began the solemn state procession from London to Windsor. Most of the mourners were paid to attend and the numbers were artificially swollen with the ranks of his servants and domestic staff who were made to wear special black outfits and walk with the body all the way to Windsor.

His lead coffin, which was carried on a lavishly decorated chariot surmounted with a life-size wax effigy of Henry VIII was bedecked with his priceless golden crown, jewelled bracelets and velvet gloves adorned with rings. The figure was so realistic that many, who saw it, including the Spanish ambassador, thought that it was actually the body of the corpulent King.

Eight miles from London, Henry VIII's funeral procession stopped for the night at Syon House. It had once been one of England's most esteemed monasteries, where Henry had spent time in pilgrimage and prayer as a youth. However during the reformation, Henry had sacked it, executed one of its priests and given the monastery to his new in-laws, the Seymours, who converted it into a grand private house.

His rapidly putrefying corpse spent the night alone in the old abbey's chapel which had been so desecrated by Henry's henchmen just years before. The following morning some of the Royal retinue noticed that the lead coffin had been mysteriously damaged during the night. It transpired that the build-up of gases from the decomposing corpse had exploded overnight, causing the casket to break open and leak body fluids. Witnesses reported the overpowering rotting stench which filled the old chapel and foul-smelling liquid of *'corrupted matter of a bloody colour'* was seen dripping from the coffin and coagulating into a pool on the stone floor.

So gruesome was the sight that it was deemed necessary to effect some emergency repairs, and local plumbers were called to re-solder the coffin before it could be moved to Windsor. On the evidence of one of these plumbers as well as other witnesses, we know that when the King's casket was being repaired, a dog, possibly belonging to one of the plumbers, ran under the coffin and began to lap from the pool of Henry's congealed pus.

One eye witness account related;

'The pavement of the church was wetted with Henry's blood. In the morning came plumbers to solder the coffin under whose feet was suddenly seen a dog creeping and licking up the King's blood. If you ask me how I know this, I answer William Grenville, who could scarcely drive away the dog told me, and so did the plumber also....'

Thus the prediction of Friar Peto came to pass in this final grotesque ignominy for the King, whose own Jezebel had driven him to countless acts of mayhem and murder against his own people. Perhaps it is little wonder that his spirit remains restless in the afterlife and continues to stalk the Castle after dark.

Anne Boleyn

Queen Anne Boleyn is one of the most famous and tragic figures in English history. Executed by her tyrannical husband, Henry VIII, on trumped-up charges of adultery and treason, for failing to provide him with a male heir, her restless spirit haunts many Royal residences. Windsor Castle is no exception and her nocturnal phantom form has been seen roaming around the Dean's Cloisters of St Georges' Chapel near to where her husband's remains are interred. One fanciful legend claims she has been seen running, holding her head firmly under her arm.

More typically, the ghostly figure has most often been seen peering from a window at the Deanery with a sad and distressed face and she has occasionally been reported weeping. So strong has been the association of this location with Anne Boleyn's ghost, that this charming bow window has now taken her name.

Although Queen Anne is perhaps best remembered for her execution at the

Engraving of Anne Boleyn by Wencelas Hollar.
Wikimedia Commons

Tower of London in 1536, she is known to have had early connections with Windsor Castle and the Dean's Cloister through her uncle who was Canon to the Chapel of St George. She is believed to have lived happily with him for a while at the Castle during her childhood, possibly sitting at this very window awaiting his return from the Chapel.

Queen Elizabeth I

The ghost of Queen Elizabeth, Anne Boleyn's daughter, is probably the most-often seen Royal phantom at Windsor Castle. It was a favourite residence of the Virgin Queen and she made many improvements to the fabric of the building. Indeed it is at the very places which were touched by her in life, that are haunted by her in death. The Royal Library was originally a long gallery which looks out onto the terraces around the Castle. This was created at her request to allow her perambulate and contemplate the affairs of state. An early account describes her daily routine;

'...she walk'd for the generality, near an hour every day before dinner, if not prevented by windy weather, to which she had a peculiar aversion. Wet weather was no manner of interruption to her amusement there; for she took great delight in walking abroad when the rain was only mild and calm with an umbrella over her head.'

Perhaps this explains why the spectral figure of the Tudor Queen has so often been seen in the Library or near these terraces. King George lll not only saw her, he talked to her. He encountered the *'stony-faced and haggard'* Queen in the library where she allegedly introduced herself to him as Elizabeth and told him that she *'was married to England.'*

The Empress Frederick of Germany, eldest daughter of Queen Victoria, declared that she saw the ghost of Elizabeth in the Library when she was a child.

Her brother Edward Vll told his mistress that he had seen a ghost at the Castle. He described her dressed all in black stating she resembled *'The Great*

Tudor Queen'.

Edward VIII when he was a young Prince of Wales was known to have had a keen interest in the occult and is rumoured to have visited mediums. His ghost hunts at the Castle were legendary and it is claimed that he witnessed a phantom apparition after an all-night vigil in the Royal Library in 1927, from which he was reported emerging *'very pale and serious.'*

His great aunt, Princess Louise is one of those who believed implicitly in the ghost of the library having received *'accounts of its appearance directly from persons who had seen it.'*

King Edward VIII's great aunt Princess Beatrice, who appears to have been psychically sensitive, saw the ghost of Elizabeth I during her childhood and on several occasions throughout her life. She once saw the figure of Gloriana standing on the terrace of the Castle. She described her as quite motionless and simply vanished after a few moments.

On another occasion the Princess was sitting quietly in her room late one night during one of her periodical visits to Castle, when her black cat, a constant companion suddenly stood up on the open window ledge and arched its back as it stared at something outside. As the Princess looked out of the window to see what had caused this unusual behaviour, she saw on the terrace two storeys below, a dark female form hurrying by. She saw the glimmer of stiff brocades in the moonlight then the spectral figure suddenly vanished. The cat leapt off the windowsill in panic dislocating its shoulder. Years later in 1897, Princess Beatrice, was reported to have changed her bedroom after a visit by the ghost of Queen Elizabeth in the middle of the night.

Her niece, Princess Alice (Countess of Athlone) was born at the Castle and whilst staying there before the First World War reported that a woman in black appeared in the suite in which she was staying. One of her children also reported during that stay that *'a black lady'* had looked in at the child while she was in bed.

These were not isolated occurrences and many distinguished guests at the Castle have endured similar nocturnal visitations over the years but have chosen to remain tight-lipped on the subject. It was known that several had even sworn their servants to silence on pain of dismissal, if they dared speak about the phantom sightings.

Some have suggested that the wraith of Elizabeth is a harbinger of disaster and appears only when England is in danger. Indeed it was reported that George VI saw the ghost of Queen Elizabeth I on eight consecutive nights in the run up to the Second World War. However not all sightings have appeared in times of crisis. His daughter the late Princess Margaret, reported seeing the apparition of Elizabeth I wandering through the Royal Library late one night. Elizabeth's materialisations can never be predicted and apparently appear only on certain nights.

The most celebrated sighting of Elizabeth however occurred in the midst of the Diamond Jubilee celebrations for Queen Victoria in 1897. She was seen in broad daylight in the Royal Library by an Officer of the Royal Guard. So much has been written about this sighting, and the story twisted both deliberately and unintentionally over the past century, that recent versions are almost unrecognisable. This story had the triple ingredients of Royalty, the supernatural and a highly credible witness, characteristics which even today are guaranteed to send the media into overdrive.

Lieutenant Arthur St Leger Glyn was a twenty-six-year-old subaltern in the 3rd Battalion Grenadier Guards stationed at Victoria Barracks in Windsor with a promising military career ahead of him. He came from a well-connected family: his father was Sidney Carr-Glyn a hero of the Crimean War and a former MP for Shaftesbury. His uncle, Edward Carr-Glyn, was the Bishop of Peterborough and his grandfather was George Carr Glyn, 1st Baronet Wolverton.

He was known to be a modest, serious and academic soldier who took his role as an officer in the elite British regiment, charged with protecting the Royal family, very seriously. Lt Glyn was well used to the responsibility of guarding Windsor Castle and one afternoon in January 1897, he took the opportunity to spend a couple of hours perusing texts in the wonderful surroundings of the Royal Library. Whilst he was there he had an experience which would catapult the unassuming young officer into newspaper headlines all around the world and cause much of the establishment to ridicule his claims of having seen something supernatural at the Castle.

The story was not in fact made public by Lt Glyn himself, but was leaked by an unknown source – possibly the Royal Librarian who was obsessed with the ghost of Elizabeth I, or possibly disclosed in innocence by the Bishop of Peterborough who was fascinated by his nephew's encounter.

The story first appeared in the 18 January edition of *Le Petit Journal* in Paris which mockingly reported that the Royal Guards had been terrified by a *'revenant'* at Windsor Castle and that Princess Beatrice had changed her bedroom because of it. Sensing this was a story with some high authority to it, the *Daily Mail* followed it up.

They dispatched a reporter to the Castle only to find that the Royal Household had departed for Osborne and the highlands and Lt Glyn was also in Islay, Scotland. It is not known whether or not this had been arranged to ensure he was unavailable or was a convenient coincidence. The Bishop of Peterborough who was also Chaplain to Queen Victoria, had already told several people about the uncanny appearance witnessed by his nephew, and had also gone abroad. Although there were many rumours circulating around the town about the sighting, reporters found lips were tightly sealed at the Castle.

On Saturday 6 February they eventually managed to track down Lt Glyn's French mother the Honourable Francoise Carr-Glyn who to their surprise confirmed that there was truth in the rumour. She went on to say;

'It is perfectly true that my son has witnessed some thing abnormal. He was, he tells me, sitting in the library of Windsor Castle reading a book; "The History of Dorsetshire" to be exact. As he read, he became aware of someone passing in the inner library. He looked up and saw a female figure in black, with black lace on the head, falling on to the shoulders. The figure passed across the library towards a corner which was out of view as my son sat, and he did not take much, notice, thinking it was somebody reading in the inner room.

This was just upon four in the afternoon, and an attendant soon afterwards came up to close the place. My son asked who the lady was who was at work in the inner room, and the attendant replied that no-one else was in the library. My son assured the attendant that a lady had just before walked across the inner room. "Then where could she be?" asked the attendant having ascertained that nobody was in the inner room. 'She must have gone out of a door in the corner,' said my son, indicating a corner to which the figure had passed. "But there is no door," said the attendant.

My son said nothing about this incident, and did not think much about it, I understand, until Mr Holmes, the librarian, asked him about it, the attendant having mentioned the matter to Mr Holmes. Asked by Mr Holmes to describe the figure he had seen, my son did so, and Mr Holmes replied that my son had seen the apparition of Queen Elizabeth.

Mr Holmes added that there were records that this apparition haunted these rooms, but Lieutenant Glyn was the first man in our time who had seen it. The Dean of Windsor also asked my son about it, and several members of the Royal Family have interviewed him on the subject. As for Mr Holmes, I am given to understand that he has spent nights and days in the library since, in the hopes of being vouchsafed a visitation.'

At that point they were joined by the Honourable Sidney Carr Glyn who upon realising the topic under conversation sprang to his defence adding;

'If my son says he has seen anything, you may take it from us that he has seen it. He is a fresh honest English boy, only a Subaltern, but fond of field sports, like most guardsmen, and unlike some guardsmen, fond of reading. He wouldn't exaggerate anything a hair's breadth.'

On Sunday night a telegram was dispatched to the young Lieutenant by his parents, soliciting leave to give the story to the *Daily Mail* on his authority. By the following morning they received the somewhat understated and bemused reply –

'Certainly, if you like. – Glyn, Grenadiers, Islay.'

The *Daily Mail* sought confirmation from the Royal Librarian, Mr (later Sir)

Richard Rivington Holmes. It was he who had been quickly alerted to the sighting by the library assistant. Mr Holmes had a keen interest in the para-normal and was all too aware of the haunted history of the Library. During his twenty-seven years as Royal Archivist, he had spent many fruitless nights in the Library hoping to see the Royal spectre and yet here was an apparently disinterested witness who had seen her in broad daylight without even trying.

When shown the sealed room from where the mysterious figure had vanished, Mr Holmes confirmed that there was indeed once a doorway leading from that room out onto the North Terrace which had been regularly used by Queen Elizabeth.

He had anxiously questioned Lt Glyn about the sighting and having heard the description escorted him to a bust of Queen Elizabeth in the library and told him that he had seen the ghost of *Good Queen Bess*. At no time before this had Lt Glyn suggested it was the shade of Elizabeth that he had seen, indeed given her iconic imagery, it is surprising that she was not instantly recognised. There is nothing to suggest that Lt Glyn gasped in shock when he saw the resemblance, if there was one, or even concurred with the conclusion made by the envious Royal Librarian.

However he did not disagree with the identification and appeared content to accept the explanation proffered by Mr Holmes. Some scholars have since suggested that the absence of her trademark pleated ruff meant the apparition was highly unlikely to have been Queen Elizabeth, as she was known never to have left her dressing room without it.

The *Daily Mail* reporter later wrote of the Royal Librarian;

'*Mr Holmes says that this gallery has had the reputation of being haunted by the ghost of Queen Elizabeth from time out of memory. His own recollection of the story dates from 27 years ago, and he has been in the habit of spending Hallowe'en in the gallery for several years in the hope of encountering her deceased Majesty.*

He had heard some rumour to the effect that the Empress Frederick had, when a child, seen an apparition in the gallery, and on her visiting Windsor next week hopes to secure some corroboration or denial of the rumour'

This corroboration was never forthcoming. By the time news had reached the Royal Family that the *Daily Mail* had the story and had been allowed access to the Library, a rear-guard action was launched. Mr Holmes was left in no doubt that he had over-stepped the mark and had his knuckles firmly rapped. The *Daily Mail* reporter, who, as agreed, had sent the draft of his copy to Mr Holmes for approval, received the curt reply from him that it was '*Unauthorised and Incorrect*'. He declined to comment any further – clearly the result of a Royal gagging order.

Nevertheless the story broke on Tuesday 9 February 1897 as a *Daily Mail* exclusive and the ensuing publicity created a storm as Windsor became the centre of a media feeding frenzy. Lt Glyn was castigated in some corners as '*a gullible fool*' and '*unhinged*'. The unwarranted attention and speculation about his mental health began to jeopardise his position as he became the subject of increasing ridicule and derision.

The Royal Family were said to be furious and refused to be drawn into any discussion about it. There seems little doubt that pressure was brought to bear on the young officer by senior figures to comment no further on the matter for fear of bringing the regiment into disrepute and embarrassing Queen Victoria. He did not however retract his story and continued to stand by every word, although never repeated it publicly for the rest of his life.

It is clear from the evidence that he was not a publicity-seeker or given to flights of fancy. At worst he was guilty of a little naivety, and in the media maelstrom which followed, probably regretted his decision to authorise the release to the *Daily Mail*. This was however the dawn of the invasive British press who as the nineteenth century drew to a close, would no longer kowtow to the Establishment in the way that it had. The story ran for months and was telegraphed all round the world. For decades later it was revived, embellished and retold to fill column inches every Halloween and Christmas. Eventually, however things settled down for Lt Glyn who rode the storm and went on to have a successful army career, surviving the Great War and retiring as a highly respected Lieutenant Colonel.

He died at Holbrook Hall in Suffolk at the age of fifty-two years on 30 November 1922, the last known witness to have seen the ghost of Elizabeth I.

King Charles I

The ghost of Charles I has been seen on several occasions during the centuries that have passed since his premature death. On one occasion he was seen in the Royal Library by a visitor to the Castle, stroking his beard in a pensive mood and leaning on the back of a chair.

The Royal Library was also the location of a famous sighting of the Cavalier King by Princess Victoria, the eldest daughter of Queen Victoria and the sighting was recorded in her diary. She was spending Easter at the Castle in her capacity as Empress having been married to Frederick Emperor of Germany. She went into the Royal Library to read after lunch. It was one of her favourite places in the Castle. It was a bright sunny day and dusty sunlight streamed in through the tall windows and flickered across the glass-fronted bookcases which line the walls, floor to ceiling. As she settled down into a leather armchair with an ancient illuminated text she suddenly became aware that someone had silently entered the room. As she looked up she saw, near the door, the figure of a gentleman, dressed in the attire of the Cavaliers standing

Charles I by Anthony Van Dyke 1635. Wikimedia Commons

as if meditating. When he raised his head and turned his face towards her, she recognised the figure at once as that of King Charles I. The figure was quite still and had a calm, smiling expression. For a moment they exchanged glances, then the Empress blinked and the figure vanished. The Empress recorded that the figure bore a strong resemblance to the Van Dyke paintings of the ill-fated Stuart monarch.

According to a former Dean of Windsor, William Boyd Carpenter, the ghost of the beheaded monarch is reported to visit an ancient house in the Canon's Close. During the first decade of twentieth century, Mrs Boyd-Carpenter, occupied this house with her husband. She stated that one day on 26 of June, she heard the ghost walk upstairs and open a bedroom door, but did not see it. Afterwards she learned that 26 June was the date on which the unhappy monarch was reputed to visit the house every year. Her husband, who was also Bishop of Ripon, was a firm believer in the Castle ghosts and went on to become an early President of the Society for Psychical Research.

In terms of witness credibility, the wife of the Archbishop of Canterbury comes high up on the list, as indeed does the daughter of an Archbishop. Edith Davidson qualified on both counts being daughter of Archbishop Archibald Tait and the wife of Archbishop Randall Davidson, a favourite of Queen Victoria and who presided at her funeral.

During the early years of the reign of Edward VII, Mrs. Davidson was staying at the Castle with her husband when she saw the distinctive and diminutive figure of Charles I pass through the cloister of the Deanery. Mrs Davidson a well-educated and pious woman gave testimony that the ghost appeared on the evening of 30 January which was the anniversary of his execution. Her account was corroborated by a number of other witnesses to whom the unfortunate King had likewise appeared over the years.

The Ghoulish Exhumation of Charles I
In Georgian Mayfair the distinguished dinner party guests at the elegant home of Sir Henry Halford looked on with intense curiosity as their host carefully passed around a small, beautifully crafted lignum vitae box. The celebrated Royal Physician took pride in his eccentric collection, but this was his most prized object. On the box, an inscription revealed the origin of the macabre contents of bone, hair and teeth.

'See the very neck bone of King Charles I, alas cut off by iron
(a sword) in 1648 and in addition the Royal Beard.'

How these bizarre Royal relics came to be at the Curzon Street home of a former physician to George III is a fascinating and ghoulish story, which has courted controversy for over 200 years. It begins with the death of King Charles I who was executed at Whitehall Palace on 30 January 1649 at the age of forty-eight. (Changes in the Gregorian calendar account for discrepancies in the date.) He was the only British monarch ever to have been beheaded. After his execution, his body was taken to St James's Palace where it lay in state for several days. On 7 February the body was brought on a boat along the Thames in a heavy snowstorm and with little ceremony for burial at Windsor.

Local legend has it that his head was stitched back onto his body on the kitchen table in the Deanery, although this is known to be untrue as the embalming was carried out when the beheaded Sovereign returned to St James's Palace from the executioner's block. On arrival at Windsor, his body was taken to the Deanery whilst a final resting place was located. The coffin was opened and inspected by a Parliamentary nobleman to confirm it was indeed the Royal corpse.

The government of Oliver Cromwell had refused King Charles a Royal burial at Westminster Abbey fearing it would invite public pilgrimage. Royalists on the other hand, feared that Roundhead extremists might further desecrate the body of the decapitated King and even mount his head on a pike at the Castle. The interment of the Sovereign was therefore done swiftly and in secret by his most loyal followers. His final resting place was to be kept a closely guarded secret to avoid his tomb being violated.

Sir Thomas Herbert, the King's faithful valet who remained with him throughout his incarceration was one of the few entrusted with the secret, and the precise location of the King's earthly remains was not discovered until a diary entry was found after long Herbert's own death. During the destruction caused to St George's Chapel during the Commonwealth, many memorials and plaques were lost and the precise whereabouts of the Royal grave became uncertain. His son Charles II tried to locate it in order to give his father a state burial at Westminster Abbey but despite many efforts to locate the tomb, he was unable to do so. Instead he spent the vast sums of money granted by Parliament for his father's mausoleum, on other things.

For over a century and a half, the whereabouts of the tomb of the martyred King remained a mystery. Then in 1813 during the construction of a mausoleum for King George III's sister Augusta, Duchess of Brunswick, in St George's Chapel, workmen accidentally broke through into a vault which contained three coffins. The largest was assumed to belong to Henry VIII, a smaller one was thought to contain the body of his third wife Jane Seymour, and a third coffin covered in a black pall was suspected of containing the long-lost body of Charles I. The Prince Regent (later George IV) saw this as an opportunity to finally identify the resting place of the King and gave permission for the coffin to be opened.

On 1 April 1813, for the first time in over 160 years, the coffin was opened in the presence of the Prince Regent and an intimate group which included the Dean of Windsor and the Royal Surgeon, Sir Henry Halford.

The following is a contemporary account of the Royal exhumation written by Sir Henry Halford.

'The vault is covered by an arch, half a brick in thickness, is seven feet two inches in width, nine feet six inches in length, and four feet ten inches in height, and is situated in the centre of the choir, opposite the eleventh knight's stall, on the sovereign's side.

On removing the pall, a plain leaden coffin, with no appearance of ever having been enclosed in wood, and bearing an inscription 'King Charles, 1648,' in large, legible characters, on a scroll of lead encircling it, immediately presented itself to the view. A square opening was then made in the upper part of the lid, of such dimensions as to admit a clear insight into its contents. These were, an internal wooden coffin, very much decayed, and the body carefully wrapped up in cere-cloth, into the folds of which a quantity of unctuous or greasy matter mixed with resin, as it seemed, had been melted, so as to exclude, as effectually as possible, the external air. The coffin was completely full; and from the tenacity of the cere-cloth, great difficulty was experienced in detaching it successfully from the parts which it enveloped. Wherever the unctuous matter had insinuated itself, the separation of the cerecloth was easy; and when it came off, a correct impression of the features to which it had been applied was observed in the unctuous substance. At length, the whole face was disengaged from its covering. The complexion of the skin of it was dark and discoloured. The forehead and temples had lost little or nothing of their muscular substance; the cartilage of the nose was gone; but the left eye, in the first moment of exposure, was open and full, though it vanished almost immediately: and the pointed beard, so characteristic of the period of the reign of King Charles, was perfect. The shape of the face was a long oval; many of the teeth remained; and the left ear, in consequence of the interposition of the unctuous matter between it and the cerecloth, was found entire.

It was difficult, at this moment, to withhold a declaration, that, notwithstanding its disfigurement, the countenance did bear a strong resemblance to the coins, the busts, and especially to the pictures of King Charles I by Vandyke, by which it had been made familiar to us. It is true, that the minds of the spectators of this interesting sight were well prepared to receive this impression; but it is also certain, that such a facility of belief had been occasioned by the simplicity and truth of Mr Herbert's narrative, every part of which had been confirmed by the investigation, so far as it had advanced: and it will not be denied that the shape of the face, the forehead, an eye, and the beard, are the most important features by which resemblance is determined.

When the head had been entirely disengaged from the attachments which confined it, it was found to be loose and, without any difficulty, was taken up and held to view. It was quite wet, and gave a greenish red tinge to paper and to linen which touched it. The back part of the scalp was entirely perfect, and had a remarkably fresh appearance; the pores of the skin being more distinct, as they usually are when soaked in moisture; and the tendons and ligaments of the neck were of considerable substance and firmness. The hair was thick at the back part of the head, and, in appearance, nearly black. A portion of it, which has since been cleaned and dried, is of a beautiful dark brown colour. That of the beard was a redder brown. On the back part of the head it was more than an inch in length, and had probably been cut so short for the convenience of the executioner or perhaps by the piety of friends soon after death, in order to furnish memorials of the unhappy King.

On holding up the head, to examine the place of separation from the body, the muscles of the neck had evidently retracted themselves considerably; and the fourth cervical vertebra was found to be cut through its substance transversely, leaving the surfaces of the divided portions perfectly smooth and even, an appearance which could have been produced only by a heavy blow, inflicted with a very

Satirical cartoon by Cruikshank of the opening of the tomb of Charles I and Henry VIII in 1813 © Royal Pavilion Museums, Brighton & Hove

sharp instrument, and which furnished the last proof wanting to identify King Charles the First.

After this examination of the head, which served every purpose in view, and without examining the body below the neck, it was immediately restored to its situation, the coffin was soldered up again, and the vault closed.

Neither of the other coffins had any inscription upon them. The larger one, supposed on good grounds to contain the remains of King Henry VIII., measured six feet ten inches in length, and had been enclosed in an elm one of two inches in thickness: but this was decayed, and lay in small fragments near it. The leaden coffin appeared to have been beaten in by violence about the middle; and a considerable opening in that part of it exposed a mere skeleton of the king. Some beard remained upon the chin, but there was nothing to discriminate the personage contained in it.

The smaller coffin, understood to be that of Queen Jane Seymour, was not touched; mere curiosity not being considered, by the Prince Regent, as a sufficient motive for disturbing these remains.'

There was no doubt that the tomb of the Charles I had at last been re-discovered. It is worthy of note that the assembled dignitaries resisted any ghoulish urge to disturb the tombs of Henry VIII or Jane Seymour, demonstrating that due reverence and Royal decorum was observed throughout the exhumation. It is surprising therefore that three items from Charles I's coffin managed to end up in Sir Henry Halford's collection of curiosities namely part of his severed fourth half-vertebra, a tooth and a piece of his reddish-brown beard.

When asked about their origin by his grandson many years later, and after the death of any witnesses to the contrary, Sir Henry claimed that the three items had been overlooked when the tomb was re-sealed. The Prince Regent allegedly said that it was not worth re-opening the coffin, and handing them to Halford said;

'…these are more in your line than mine, you had better keep them.'

Controversy has reigned ever since, with some medical professionals accusing Sir Henry of purloining the relics whilst others claim, this would not have been possible with the number of people present. Furthermore the piece of paper which accompanied the artefacts, bore the address of the Dean of Windsor who allegedly gave it to him to wrap them in.

Whatever the truth, With the death of Sir Henry, his grandson Sir Henry St John Halford, the third baronet, inherited the relics. He and his brother had no heirs and were concerned as to what might become of them. Halford's grandson decided that they should be returned to the Royal family. In 1888 The Prince of Wales received the relics, apparently with some trepidation and with Queen Victoria's permission the relics were replaced in the coffin of King Charles I. The Dean of Windsor had a leaden casket prepared which bore the following inscription:

'The relics in this case were taken from the coffin of King Charles I on April 1st 1813, by Sir Henry Halford, Physician to King George III. They were by his grandson Sir Henry St. John Halford given to H.R.H. Albert Edward, Prince of Wales. On December 13th 1888 they were replaced by H.R.H. in this vault, their original resting place.'

Queen Anne

Queen Anne was born at Windsor and spent much of her reign there. She is supposed to haunt the Royal Library. It was in the alcoves of the Library that she heard the news of Marlborough's decisive victory over the French at the Battle of Blenheim in 1704, but recent sightings of her ghost are few and far between.

The ghost of a woman *'in a little brown dress'* has been seen by many people who work at the Royal Archives. Her presence has been described as *'friendly'* and her appearances do nothing to alarm those who have seen her, although there is nothing to suggest that this has anything to do with the eighteenth-century Queen.

There is however a curious and ancient superstition which is still observed by the Royal family which re-ignited during the Queen's reign.

Anne was plagued by ill-health throughout her life and grew increasingly lame and obese from a relatively young age. Despite seventeen pregnancies by her husband, Prince George of Denmark, she died without any surviving children and the House of Stuart died with her. Her inability to bear children revived the centuries-old superstition that Windsor was cursed and that no Royal children could be born at the Castle. This legend began 700 years ago during the time of Edward III, the first King born at Windsor. His son, the Black Prince died before coming to the throne which gave rise to a belief that any heir born there would die prematurely or be otherwise ill-fated. A strange prophesy was made about it by Henry V. When the news came to him that his wife had borne a son at Windsor Castle, it is known that he said;

'Henry born at Monmouth shall small time reign and much get, but Henry born at Windsor shall long reign and lose all. As God wills- let it be.'

Henry V reigned only nine years and conquered France as a military hero while his son Henry VI reigned thirty-nine years, lost France, went out of his mind and saw the beginnings of the Wars of the Roses.

Since this time successive Royal dynasties, including the present one, have deliberately avoided having their children born at Windsor Castle for fear of resurrecting the ancient curse.

King George III

King George III was on the throne for almost sixty years, and was the longest reigning King of England. Only Victoria and Elizabeth II have since reigned longer. Known as 'Farmer George' for his love of agriculture, George was a handsome and cultured monarch and committed family man. Sadly he is best remembered for losing the American colonies and descending into madness during the latter part of his reign.

His madness (now diagnosed as a symptom of the kidney disorder porphyria) became so severe that in 1811 he became permanently incapable and his eldest son was made Prince Regent. In 1818 his wife Charlotte died and George lived out the rest of his days detained at Windsor Castle as he descended further into insanity. He was confined for his own protection to a set of rooms above the Royal Library. Often he could be heard screaming behind the locked doors or rambling incoherently, once for fifty-eight hours non-stop, and yet during periods of lucidity he would play Handel on his harpsichord.

On Easter bank holiday in 1930 the Royal family were in the print room of the Library overlooking the North Terrace when King George V related the story of the ghost of George III who had been confined to that very room for the last ten years of his life. Indeed he was to die there at the age of eighty-one on 29 January 1820. In happier days he would often call in members of the guard and serve them hot punch and beer. At the end of his life, although he was very confused, he would never miss the changing of the guard which took place beneath his bedroom window. On hearing the command *'Eyes Right'*, he would raise his hand in acknowledgment to the guard commander. This became a regular pattern for the deranged old King.

After his death in 1820, whilst his body lay in his coffin in St George's Chapel prior to his funeral, the guard change continued as usual. Out of habit, the guard commander looked up at the King's window and was startled to see a pair of pale hands part the curtain and the bearded and dishevelled figure of the old King appear at the glass As he gave the command *'Eyes Right'* the ghostly figure once again raised his arm in acknowledgement.

The young guard commander went on to become Sir William Knollys, Comptroller to King Edward VII and told this story to George V in his youth. The story was captured in the guide to Windsor Castle written by the Royal Librarian Sir Owen Morshead in 1951.

After this famous sighting, rumours of the ghost of 'mad' King George became rife and he was seen again at this window and elsewhere in the Castle. Royal guards came to dread their posting to the North Terrace and even battle-hardened veterans reported a sense of unease when working there. Other witnesses have heard the disembodied voice of the phantom roaming the corridors muttering a phrase he was fond of saying while alive, *'What, What?'*

There was a persistent rumour throughout the 1930s that a living member of the Royal family had refused to visit Windsor for over three decades because she once encountered a horrifying ghost which frightened her half to death. There was much speculation about the family member whose identity was never disclosed, but the ghost was believed to be that of George III who appeared in the Royal Library as an insane and frightening old man.

Whilst he had a miserable end to his life, many who had seen him reported that his shade appears happy and smiling in death. The ghost appeared finally just before the death of William IV in 1837 and with the demise of the Hanoverian dynasty, the mournful ghost of 'mad' King George apparently disappeared for good.

However a remarkable sighting took place during the reign of Queen Victoria. A titled lady walking through one of the picture galleries in Windsor Castle one day noticed an old gentleman standing gazing very intently at a portrait. Curious to see why he was so intrigued, she went up to it and saw that it was a portrait of George III with nothing, so far as the lady could see, remarkable about it. She was wondering what made the gentleman by her side so interested in it, when he suddenly remarked;

'*How little has really ever been published about him, and what a lot that mouth could tell, had it but the power of speech.*'

He then went on to regale the woman with many extraordinary incidents about the life of George III which were so fantastic and absurd that it was with the greatest difficulty that she refrained from laughing out loud. Nevertheless she politely listened and humoured him.

He concluded by saying:

'*He could live forever - and they say he was mad, but the maddest thing he ever did was to die, when with his incomparable intellect and all he knew, he could undoubtedly have lived forever.*'

Muttering incoherently to himself the gentleman then walked away and it was at this point that the woman noticed for the first time that he was wearing strangely old-fashioned attire, more like that worn many years ago in the days of her grandfather. Wondering who he could be she followed him at a distance, and saw him pass through a doorway at which an official of the Castle was on duty. Going up to the official she asked: '*Who was that gentleman that just passed by.*'

'*When?*' the official replied, looking rather puzzled. '*Why, just now, a moment ago,*' the lady answered.

The official then asked the woman to describe the man. When she did so the official turned pale and exclaimed in trembling tones; '*Why, that was the ghost the servants have often spoken to me about, and which, for some reason or another, I never can see.*'

'*Who is it supposed to be?*' the lady inquired. '*No one knows*' was the response, '*...but the odd part about it is that, although, judging from its appearance, it is not the ghost of George III, it always appears about the time of year he died and apparently takes the greatest interest in him. Some think it must be the ghost of some near relative of his, who, for some peculiar reason, history does not mention.*'

The lady reported that she never saw the apparition again and the identity of this ghostly Georgian gentleman remains a mystery.

Queen Victoria

The last known Royal to haunt Windsor is Queen Victoria. Although she appears to be happily reunited her beloved Prince Albert, her ghost did make a rare daytime appearance during Edward's VIII's brief reign in 1936.

A short time after the death of George V, Edward started to modify the Windsor Castle grounds at the direction of his lover, Wallace Simpson, for whom he later abdicated the throne. She requested several spruce trees be removed that Queen Victoria and Prince Albert had planted. As the workmen proceeded to cut down these trees, several inexplicable incidents occurred that hampered their work, including tools becoming lost and malfunctioning. The final straw came when the workmen saw the unmistakeable figure of Queen Victoria's displeased ghost running from the direction of the Castle towards them, moaning loudly and waving her arms frantically. The terrified workers fled the scene and reported back to the King who though better of the plans and decided to leave the trees alone. She has not been seen since.

In recent years rumours have circulated that Queen Victoria used a medium to channel messages from the grave from her dead husband. On at least one occasion she is known to have withdrawn from a Privy Council meeting to consult with the dead Albert and when she returned, declared that *'The Prince was hostile to any act of war by England.'*

Queen Victoria's grief was legendary and she remained in mourning for her Prince Consort for forty years. She was known to have an interest in the occult and supernatural. In her youth when the fashionable craze of spiritualism swept across the Atlantic from the United States, she held a séance at Osborne House in July 1846 using the clairvoyant Georgiana Eagle, who gave a demonstration of her powers to the Royal couple

So when Albert died unexpectedly of typhoid from the Windsor drains in 1861, just months after her mother's death, Victoria was inconsolable. Her

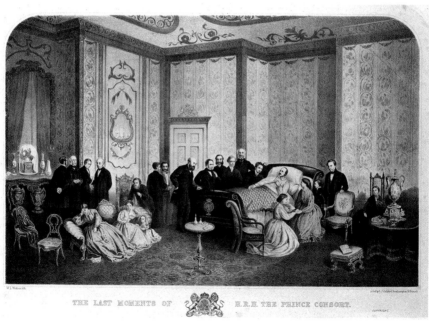

Death of Prince Albert in the Blue Room at Windsor Castle 1861.
Wellcome Library, London

greatest wish was that she should die and join him and she became convinced she could hear his voice.

It has been claimed that after his death Victoria regularly held séances in the sumptuous Blue Room at Windsor Castle where he drew his last breath. The room was kept as a shrine for four decades. Each night a clean nightshirt was laid out for him as it had been in life. Fresh flowers and a jug of hot water were ritually prepared and it is known that Victoria took a pair of his woollen pants to bed with her every night.

Although never officially confirmed, it is not difficult to imagine the distraught Victoria availing herself of whatever means possible, including a clairvoyant medium, in an effort to hear his voice again.

Stories have emerged that shortly after Albert's death Victoria heard that a thirteen-year-old medium Robert James Lees had held a séance in Birmingham during which the spirit of the dead Albert had apparently spoken through him. She dispatched two undercover courtiers to examine the claims. To the courtiers' amazement, they heard Lees speaking in a voice unmistakably that of the Prince consort. Stranger still, he addressed the courtiers by their real names, not their pseudonyms. And he knew many private details about Victoria's life that only Albert could have known. The stunned courtiers hurried back to tell the Queen about their experiences.

Lees then sent a letter to the Queen, purportedly written by Albert and signed with a pet name used only between Albert and his wife. This prompted Victoria to invite the boy medium to conduct nine séances during which it is alleged that Albert spoke to her through him. It is claimed that Victoria offered Lees the post of Royal Medium in residence but he declined on the advice of his spirit guide. He did however reassure her that Albert had chosen another medium through which he would contact her whom he described as; 'The boy who used to carry my gun at Balmoral.'

This 'boy' (although he was in his late thirties) was John Brown, whom Albert had appointed as Victoria's personal ghillie, or hunting guide, at Balmoral and who was said to have posessed psychic powers. These were once demonstrated when he wished the Royal party well on their departure from Balmoral in autumn 1861. He said that he hoped they would all return safe 'and above all that you may have no deaths in the family.' Within a week King Pedro of Portugal and Prince Ferdinand died and Prince Albert followed a few weeks later. This convinced Victoria that Brown was possessed of second sight.

Brown was brought down from the Highlands and although courtiers were pleased that he appeared to coax the Queen out of her depression, they quickly became concerned that she had fallen entirely under his spell and he was exerting undue influence upon her.

He soon became her closest and most-trusted confidante, consulted on every

Queen Victoria and Prince Albert 1854.
Wikimedia Commons

aspect of her life including state affairs. This has led to speculation that Brown was indeed regularly channelling the spirit of the dead Prince and explains why the couple became so inseparable that she was mockingly referred to as 'Mrs Brown.'

It is believed that Victoria, a life-long diarist kept a private journal of the séances which were destroyed after her death along with her intimate letters to her 'Darling Brown.' It has been claimed that King George VI once found a record of a séance which had been overlooked at the back of a drawer but this has been officially denied.

It is however known that after her death, Victoria's personal doctor, Sir James Reid, had to intervene in a case of blackmail, involving a cache of 300 'most compromising' letters she had written to her estate manager at Balmoral, Dr Profeit, in which she reportedly discussed her interest in communicating with the other world through Brown. Sir James purchased the letters on behalf of her son Edward VII, who destroyed them.

Further evidence may have existed in the affectionate memoir Victoria wrote about John Brown after his death in 1883. Her senior courtiers however, refused to let her publish it, fearing that it would further damage her reputation, and had it destroyed, together with Brown's own diaries.

It would seem that any proof of Victoria's communication with the ghost of Prince Albert has gone with her to the grave.

Chapter 3
WHO GOES THERE ?

THERE ARE STORIES stretching back centuries of Royal guards being terrified by nocturnal visitations. Ghostly apparitions have often been cited as the reasons for people fleeing the Castle in the middle of the night although usually these were maids and servants rather than soldiers. One unusual case concerns Private James Richardson who mysteriously disappeared overnight whilst on sentry duty, leaving his rifle and uniform behind him.

At 11pm on Wednesday 25 August 1869 the Grenadier Guard commander was doing his usual rounds checking on the sentries posted around Windsor Castle. On the North Terrace he expected to see Private Richardson who had taken up his duty outside the Royal apartments just two hours before, but he was nowhere to be found. Fearing something untoward had happened to him, the alarm was raised and a full search was conducted which discovered his rifle and uniform in a heap where he was last seen.

His surprising disappearance led to speculation amongst some of his colleagues that he had been spirited away by ghosts. Stories were rife in the regiment of the phantoms which haunted the Castle and the night time postings on the eerie terraces around the Royal apartments were dreaded by many.

Nowadays, conspiracy theorists would have labelled this a case of alien abduction but 150 years ago, the phantom of Herne the Hunter was blamed for taking another soul for his 'wild ride'.

The Grenadier Guards were however more circumspect and treated this as a case of desertion. This was a serious military crime, particularly for a guard of the Royal Family and could be punishable by death. His colleagues were not aware of anything that would have precipitated this sudden drastic step and were baffled that he managed to leave the Castle grounds without being seen by other sentries posted in and around the grounds. His only means of escape was to make his way down The Hundred Steps from the North Terrace and into the Home Park. This desertion was unusual and caused quite a stir within the regiment and gave rise to widespread speculation in the local media about its cause.

Private Richardson was apprehended a fortnight later in London. He never gave any explanation for his unprecedented disappearance and took his punishment without complaint and expressed relief that he no longer had to guard the Castle. He was sentenced to 168 days imprisonment and branded with the letter 'D' for deserter. As well as serving as a deterrent for others, this brutal scarring was to ensure he never tried to re-enlist after discharge. What caused him to flee his post that night remains a mystery.

Discipline was harsh in Victoria's army. Although flogging had been partially abolished for most military offences in 1867 after the death of a young Private Robert Slim, it was still a sanction available for desertion. Branding was not outlawed until 1871 and was usually done on the breast or hip but for serious cases such as this it was carried out on the cheek or forehead.

Some years previously a sentry was found accused sleeping on the job whilst guarding Windsor Castle. The penalty at the time was death by firing squad but at his court martial he claimed that he was awake and had heard St Paul's clock chime thirteen at midnight. This was found to have been true and saved his life although his hearing must have been acute.

Long before Private Richardson's case, at the height of the Napoleonic wars, another sentry on duty at the North Terrace during the early hours of the morning endured a terrifying supernatural experience. On 29 September 1812 one of the Corporal's relief guards was found collapsed beneath the window of a private room under Queen Elizabeth's gallery, with musket, bayonet and cap lying by his side. Although not named, he was described as;

'…a brave fellow of the 29th regt who had served under Wellington during the Peninsular wars and had been twice wounded at Talavera in 1809.'

He was taken to the guard room and revived, and related how a gliding ghostly figure in black had approached him. He had confronted it but his challenge went unanswered. The guard again challenged the figure to stop but receiving no reply and seeing that the figure was continuing towards him, he lunged forward with his bayonet into thin air as the figure vanished. The guard terrified out of his wits screamed for help and was swiftly joined by a colleague who found him in a *'state of great alarm and agony.'*

The soldier was well known for his bravery and quickly regained his composure and expressed his embarrassment that he had reacted in such a foolish manner and asked if he could return to his post. The guard commander allowed him to resume his post but around half an hour later, they heard a blood curdling cry coming from the soldier on the North Terrace, screaming *'I am lost! I am lost!'*

They raced around the corner and found the soldier unconscious on the floor with a part of his gun broken off.

Once he recovered he was babbling incoherently and told them that the same figure had again appeared before him and had floated towards a wall where he struck it with his weapon. The gun had gone straight through the figure and broken against the stone wall as the figure disappeared before his eyes.

There was a suggestion at the time that he could have been the subject of a practical joke of an optical nature played from a nearby apartment but this was dismissed as the figure he described was '*wholly dark*' and the only apartment nearby was completely unoccupied. Nevertheless the sceptical *Windsor Express* became convinced that this was hoax, reporting that;

'*...an artist was compelled to leave his pleasant apartments carrying his phantasmagorical devices with him. It was difficult for many to comprehend that such optical deceptions were not difficult to manage.*'

Many found difficulty in accepting the result of the official investigation which concluded that on the night in question the guardsmen had been discussing '*ghost and goblins*' and that it was his imagination playing tricks on him that had caused the guardsman to hallucinate and see a ghost.

Encounters with the undead can sometimes lead to tragic consequences. On 12 December 1863 a young soldier, Private Bradshaw on duty at the entrance to the Royal Mews, attempted to commit suicide by shooting himself in the head with his service rifle. This led to conjecture amongst the ranks that he had seen the vision of a horrible spectre which caused him to take his own life. He survived for several days with horrific head injuries. In the days prior to his death he had reported seeing a ghost in the vicinity of the Castle. Some weeks after his death, a terrified guardsman, saw the smiling ghost of the dead soldier walking towards him on the Long Walk. The spectral soldier then vanished into thin air. When he finished his duty, he rushed back to his quarters, and still shaken by the experience, related the story of his awful encounter. It was then that a colleague who had been on the shift before him admitted that he too had seen the same ghost on the Long Walk that night but had been too afraid to tell for fear of being ridiculed.

In 1906 a policeman guarding Edward VII reported seeing a ghostly Grenadier, which was also witnessed by another sentry. The spectral sentry visited again in 1927 when it was seen by another night-shift guardsman on the Long Walk

In 1889 a sentry on duty on the East Terrace made an official report that he had been approached by a hooded and veiled figure of a woman who glided towards him in a most unearthly manner before falling to her knees just a few yards away in an act of supplication as if to beseech him for something. She then disappeared as though she had fallen through the ground. The terrified soldier immediately reported the matter and was initially accused of being drunk on duty. When it was discovered he patently was not, he was ordered to return to his post but was so frightened that he adamantly refused to do so, incurring the wrath of military discipline by his actions. It is reported that the otherwise '*good and sober*' soldier refused ever to do duty on the East Terrace again, such was the effect the apparition had upon him.

The ghost of an Elizabethan woman assumed to be *'Good Queen Bess'* has been sighted on many occasions, including by a sentry again on the eerie East Terrace. The sentry was found by the officer of the guard in a state of abject terror. His explanation as that a woman dressed in Elizabethan garb complete with cowl and ruff had walked to within a few paces of him and vanished before he had time to put in a challenge. Present at the Castle at the time, waiting to be deployed to the Flanders trenches, was Grenadier Guardsman Raymond Asquith, a gifted barrister and the son of the Liberal Prime Minister Herbert Asquith, who was fascinated with the supernatural and personally interviewed the soldier concerned. He was so impressed with the earnestness of the soldier, who was by all accounts experienced and not normally nervous, that he did nightly turns on the Terrace himself, in the hope of seeing the ghostly figure. He was not successful but declared that he would repeat the

The East Terrace of Windsor Castle – the scene of numerous ghostly sightings c. 1895.
Wikimedia Commons

experiment when next at the Castle. Sadly he was killed at Amiens in 1916 before he could return to Windsor,

Experiments were conducted on the East Terrace following a bizarre theory that certain lighting conditions could cause the outline of an Elizabethan painting from inside the Castle, to be projected onto the external walls. Not surprisingly this explanation was quickly discredited leaving the supernatural version to hold the field.

In 1936 a sentry is reported to have fainted when he watched the headless figure of a woman dressed all in black walk down through the Horseshoe Cloister and disappear before him. Other sentries have frequently reported the sound of raucous activity coming from parts of the Castle they know to be unoccupied.

As late as the 1950s, a sentry found in a dead faint on the East Terrace instead of being on guard outside the Royal Apartments, stated that he had seen the dark form of a woman approaching him and when his first and second challenges went unheeded he raised his rifle and was at the point of firing over her head when the figure vanished. This account, which features in the official records, was put down to an *'unexplained incident'* and the soldier avoided a court-martial as enquiries revealed that the figure had been seen by other sentries at various times.

Even in more recent times, stories continue to emerge about strange apparitions seen by sentries during their night shift. In September 1976 a Guardsman on duty on the East Terrace was found unconscious. When he recovered he claimed that one of the statutes in the Italian garden had come to life and sprouted horns and rushed towards him causing him to faint with fright. He apparently had no prior knowledge of the legend of Herne the Hunter who for centuries has haunted Windsor Great Park.

At around the same time a bizarre incident was reported by several soldiers who saw the statue of Charles II come to life and dismount his horse in the quadrangle. The incredulous soldiers watched the figure stride across the quad before it disappeared. When they looked back to the equestrian statute, the Merry Monarch had resumed his seat astride his steed. At the time this was quickly hushed up amidst rumours of drug use to counteract the long tours of duty at the Castle. No eyewitness accounts of this incident appear to exist.

Some ghostly appearances however have been properly explained and found to have quite earthly origins. One such story concerns Queen Victoria's Dean of Windsor who, one bitterly cold night, was preparing for bed and drinking a warming toddy in his nightshirt. He looked out of his bedroom window and saw a lone sentry pacing the Dean's Cloisters in an effort to keep warm. Feeling sorry for him, the Dean prepared a hot drink and went down in his night clothes to hand him the drink. The sentry saw a white disembodied arm appear from the wall and fled screaming in terror.

Such is the reputation of the Castle that it is easy to see how young Guardsmen get the 'heebie jeebies' whilst on duty there at night. It is not therefore difficult to imagine that suggestion and expectation contribute to the enormous number of sightings recorded at the Castle. We can assume that the ghostly arm would have been another addition to the ghostly chronicles had the Dean not chased after him to reassure him. It is believed that Queen Victoria *was* amused by this story.

There was less Royal hilarity however following the infamous case of Private Bentley. On Friday 2 March 1906 as King Edward VII and the Royal Family enjoyed an extended supper in the State Apartments at Windsor Castle, Private Walter Bentley of the 2nd Battalion Coldstream Guards was spending a cold night shift guarding the terrace below them. He was an experienced soldier and knew the Castle well, having performed many tours there in his service to King and Country. However that night shift was to prove an extraordinary one for Private Bentley. Within a few hours his name would be emblazoned across all the morning papers as the Royal guard who had fired off five rounds at the Windsor Castle 'ghost'.

The night shift had begun routinely enough. As the wind whistled around him, Private Bentley armed with his Lee Enfield rifle with bayonet fixed; paced along the East Terrace, anticipating the hours of tedium he had ahead of him. As the gloomy darkness and icy mist descended, he looked up at the illuminated windows of the apartments above him and could hear the faint sound of revelry coming from within. *'Bet it's a damn sight warmer up there'* he muttered. He reflected on the long journey he had made from his home town of Bradford and here he was guarding the King of England. *'If only it wasn't so bloody boring'* he said out loud to himself as he checked his pocket watch. It was 9.15pm. As he looked up, something caught his eye. Someone was moving on the terrace. No ... there was more than one person ... and they were moving towards him. With a start, he pulled his rifle round, brought it up to his shoulder and slid back the bolt.

'Halt!' he shouted, his voice cracking in nervousness *'Who goes there?'* No reply came.

As he strained to focus in the inky blackness, he could still see the figures moving relentlessly towards him. *'Halt – Who goes there?'* he repeated. *'I'm going to bloody shoot'* he warned, and with that fired a shot into one of the shadowy figures. The bullet seemed to pass right through. Private Bentley now, in a state of utter fright and panic fired off a further four shots at the marauding spectral figures before bayonet-charging them with a blood-curdling scream which echoed around the Castle walls. But nothing solid met the cold steel of his bayonet. He stopped incredulous and looked around him. *'Where the hell are they?'* he asked himself. But there was nothing with him in the cold night air. The silence was then broken by the clatter of boots running across the stone pavement from the direction of the guardroom as his night shift colleagues ran towards him. *'What's happened Wally?'* they asked breathlessly *'Who've you shot?'* Private Bentley looked around him unable to speak, the five spent brass cartridges being the only evidence of his encounter with the phantom intruders.

Within minutes Private Bentley still shaking with terror, was being frog-marched to the guardroom where he spent a night in the cells for improperly discharging his weapon.

As dawn broke, the evidence of Private Bentley's actions was plain for all to see. In the beautiful sunken flower garden laid out by George IV stood the pair of magnificent 'Lucknow' stone elephants, one of which was now adorned with five bullet holes. Major Lambton, the Commanding Officer was summoned to the Castle to explain to the Royal Household why his guards had used the prized statuary for nocturnal target practice.

The Lucknow Elephant at Windsor Castle which terrified Private Bentley in 1906
Author's Collection

On returning to Combermere Barracks, Major Lampton quickly convened a courtmartial for improper use of his weapon. Private Bentley asserted his honest belief that he was firing at intruders who refused to obey his command to halt and could not explain what had happened to them. His punishment was confinement to barracks for three days, which was a surprisingly lenient penalty given the circumstances. Does this imply his C.O. had some sympathy for what the soldier saw? Major Lambton suggested to the local newspapers that Private Bentley was normally *'a cool-headed and good soldier'* and had *'no previous history of hallucinations'* In fact Private Bentley was far from a model soldier and the Major was in all likelihood conducting a damage-limitation exercise in an effort to avoid the regiment becoming a laughing stock.

Digging deeper into the regimental records reveals that Private Bentley was a thoroughly bad lot and his testimony, regardless of how earnestly delivered, should be taken with a pinch of salt. Throughout his army career Private

Bentley displayed contempt of authority. He was absent without leave many times and on numerous occasions found drunk in the streets in a dishevelled state. He had been court-martialled several times for a variety of offences against military discipline and had deserted on more than one occasion. For some time Bentley had been on a course self-destruction. His record suggests he no longer wanted to be in the army and his indiscipline was such that it seemed he was trying his utmost get himself dismissed from the regiment. Just five weeks before the infamous 'Elephant' incident, he deserted his post whilst on sentry duty at Windsor Castle and the following day failed to turn up for duty. When challenged he made *'an improper remark'* to a superior officer. For these offences he was sentenced to ten days imprisonment with hard labour.

By 1908 Bentley's career was in tatters and he deserted the army turning to a life of crime. He was recaptured after the outbreak of the First World War but constantly deserted and in November 1916 suddenly dropped dead whilst on another crime spree. A sudden end to a turbulent and troubled life.

One explanation to his bizarre behaviour and perhaps a clue to the Windsor Castle 'ghosts', can be found in his military medical records. In 1904 Private Bentley was diagnosed with syphilis. In the advanced stages this can create mental imbalance and in many cases invoke hallucinations. Was venereal disease the cause of his downfall and does that explain his frightening night visions on the windswept East Terrace of Windsor Castle – or was it truly a supernatural experience that turned his mind?

Another ghost story was launched by the miraculous wraith of a 'dead' colleague that appeared at Victoria Barracks shortly before Hallowe'en in 1885. Trooper Grubb had been serving with the 2nd Life Guards in Sudan when he was lost in the heat of a fierce battle. His body was never recovered and he was mourned by his colleagues as a brave soldier who had made the ultimate sacrifice for Queen and Country. Imagine the reaction when months later, long after his regiment had returned back to England, the apparition of Trooper Grubb was seen walking into the guardroom at Combermere Barracks at Windsor.

The terrified guard reaching for his rifle suddenly realised that his former colleague was in fact flesh and blood ... and heavily sun-bronzed to boot. Having been separated from his unit he had tracked his way back to the Nile and with a combination of hard-riding, hard-fighting and daredevil gallantry worthy of *'Boy's Own'*, Trooper Grubb had made his way back to civilisation to rejoin his old comrades.

The mysteries behind Windsor Castle ghosts are rarely solved but in one case in 1871 an old soldier, Private William Evans, disclosed how many years before he had been a very nervous young Guardsman posted to a midnight tour of duty inside the cloisters of St George's Chapel. During that period many of his colleagues had been frightened out of their wits after seeing a horrifying apparition appear before them. So frightened were they that several had fled their posts in terror risking exemplary punishment for dereliction of duty. Alarm was spreading through the ranks with such vigour, that the Guard Commander was happy to accept an offer from Private Evans to lie in wait and prove to his colleagues that the ghost did not exist.

In his own words the plucky Guardsman related;

'Determined to elucidate the mystery, I secured the confidence of the sergeant, and was detailed to take over this particular post at the witching hour. In a secluded part of the cloisters (a most gloomy place, even in the daylight) was a door leading to the private apartments of one of the resident clerical officials. Taking up my station on the shady side of this door, I waited with bated breath, for the ghost to appear.'

After waiting silently for some time with growing anxiety, his patience was rewarded.

'Presently the door was stealthily opened, and a figure emerged entirely draped in white, and walked with ghostly strides towards the place where the sentry is usually posted. Quick as lightning I shut the door with a loud, slam, and the ghost, giving a frantic scream, flew towards it, and throwing off the white table-cloth, disclosed the bewitching form and pretty features of Mary Ann, the house-maid of the said clerical official.'

The enterprising Mary Ann had taken to frightening away the guards in order to facilitate her nocturnal rendezvous with the unnamed clerical official. Private Evans concludes in his memoire:

'It is needless to add that "mum" was the word, and since some years have elapsed, no harm can be done by the recital of how I laid to rest the 'Ghost of the Cloisters.''

One can only speculate on how many ghost stories Mary Ann and her fellow maids spawned with their midnight shenanigans around the Castle.

Chapter 4
THE GHOSTLY KNIGHTS OF WINDSOR CASTLE

SHORTLY AFTER THE end of the First World War, a gentleman known only as Mr B. was staying in the Castle in the absence of royalty. He was staying at Windsor in an official capacity and he spent an uneventful but very pleasant first night in one of the splendid bedrooms. The second night however he found it difficult to get to sleep. After lying awake for some time he finally managed to drift off, but around midnight he was suddenly awakened with a violent start.

Fancying he had heard a noise, he sat up in bed and listened, and then heard from some distance away, the sound of approaching footsteps. The sounds came rapidly nearer, and he realised that it was the sound of two persons running, but there was a curious metallic clanging and clattering that accompanied the footsteps which perplexed him very much. It seemed almost as if the two were carrying armfuls of steel helmets that kept rattling and jangling. Then it dawned on him that the runners sounded as though they were in armour!

He shook his head as if to dismiss such a foolish notion but the last shadow of doubt vanished as the clattering on the stone paved corridor came to rest outside his bedroom. Then the clash, clash, clatter of the unmistakeable sound of metal upon metal outside his bedroom door. Believing this to be a practical joke in very poor taste, especially in the early hours of the morning, Mr B. got out of bed and tiptoed over to the door and snatched it open in order to confront the perpetrators red-handed.

As he opened the door he felt a distinct but invisible force push him through it and almost fell into the corridor. The sight he beheld caused him to shrink back against the door frame in horror. In front of him were two men in full armour which he said *'shone in the darkness of the hall as though covered with phosphorus.'* Both had swords, but one also had a huge battle-axe with which he was fighting. Mr B. could hear the din of sword and axe striking against the armour. The one using the axe uttered no sound, but the groans and the panting of the swordsman were heartrending. Clearly, he was the weaker of the two and in mortal danger

Mr B. realised that he was looking upon no combat of earthly men. Suddenly, as he stared, with terror-filled eyes, the swordsman dropped to his knees, felled by a blow from the axe. He heard through the visor of the helmet a frenzied scream for mercy. Unheeding that prayer, the figure with the axe brought the blade down upon the neck, shearing through the armour and into the spectral flesh!

In an instant the two battling figures vanished. Mr B. traumatised by what he had seen, crept back into his room and locking the door, placed against it all the chairs he could find to barricade himself in. He spent the rest of the night terrified in his bed with all the lights on. Early in the morning as soon as he could hear the palace servants were moving about, he sought out a member of the Royal Household and told him his story.

The courtier listened intently, and then said:

'I am sorry, but owing to certain repairs that were going on in the new wing we had to put you in a part of the Castle that is seldom used now. It is an ancient part and has a bad reputation among some. The story is that two nobles in Henry VIII's reign, who were in love with the same woman, fought one another in that hall. I have never heard anything there, nor did I believe the story, but now I am forced to believe it and will put no other guests in any of the rooms adjoining it.'

There are no official records to corroborate this ancient fight to the death or who the noblemen were, but Mr B. needed no further proof and remained convinced to the end of his days that he had experienced a time-slip and witnessed the re-enactment of a brutal medieval murder at Windsor Castle.

Chapter 5
'BLOODY' MARY'S PHANTOM INQUISITOR

THE ANNALS OF Windsor Castle are replete with stories of ghostly apparitions and many remain buried away in the duty books kept by the Royal Household and Officer of the Watch responsible for recording significant or unexpected occurrences befalling the sentries during their tour of duty. It is very unlikely that these will ever see the light of day but what tales must be contained within them. One sinister story, allegedly from these long-forgotten accounts, concerns a visitor to the Castle during the early part of the twentieth century.

A certain Mrs Manning is said to have gone on a visit to the Castle *'during the absence of the Royal family'*. She was given a room overlooking the courtyard. It was described as a long, low rectangular apartment with nothing very noticeable in it except the bed, which was an antique four-poster. Mrs. Manning was not a nervous person, and in spite of the strangeness of the room, she got into bed quite unconcernedly and fully prepared to sleep soundly till the morning. This, however, was not to be. She awoke with a start to hear a clock from somewhere close at hand, solemnly strike one. She was surprised to see the room bathed in moonlight and every object as clearly discernible as if it had been day. A feeling of intense exhilaration seized her and she got up and went to the window, threw it wide open and leaned out. The air was wonderfully sweet, full of the scent of clover and new mown hay. She was drinking in great gulps of it with wide-open mouth, when her eyes encountered the gaze of someone peering up at her from immediately beneath the window sill.

She described the face she looked into as *'long, narrow and swarthy. It had a pointed beard and long moustaches, very much bewaxed at the ends. The eyes were dark and strangely luminous.'*

As she looked down into his eyes, the figure smiled sardonically at her. Much startled, and yet at the same time fascinated, Mrs Manning continued staring at the stranger for some seconds, and then by a supreme effort of willpower she eventually removed her gaze and slammed shut the window and returned to bed.

The next morning she mentioned the occurrence to one of the Castle officials, and inquired of him who the strange looking visitor was. The official hesitated and appeared so uncomfortable that Mrs Manning at once became curious and pressed him for an explanation. Seeing there was no way out of it the official at length told her.

'What you saw in the night was undoubtedly one of the apparitions that periodically haunt the Castle grounds. It is generally believed to be the ghost of a member of the cruel Spanish Inquisition, who is rumoured to have resided here for a while during the reign of 'Bloody' Mary. So long as he only looks at you, it is alright but should he touch you dire consequences invariably follow.'

Mrs Manning a level-headed modern woman had never believed in ghosts before, but was now convinced that what she had seen was actually something supernatural. She made it known to the staff that nothing would induce her to go out after dark during the remainder of her stay.

Queen 'Bloody' Mary Tudor by Hans Holbein. Wikimedia Commons

Two days later, however, she received a invitation to dine with some friends at nearby Slough. Had she been going alone she would probably have refused, but was cajoled into accepting by several others who were also staying at the Castle.

The evening was a great success, during the course of which Mrs Manning shared her experience with her companions who found it highly entertaining. By the time they started back for Windsor it was dark but they were in high spirits and it was fine clear moonlit night

All was well until they entered the Castle grounds and were walking along a lonely path bordered on either side by lofty trees and shrubs. One of the party then suddenly shrieked that they had seen someone hiding in the trees.

This aroused the curiosity of the rest of the group who halted and looked around them. Nothing however was to be seen apart from trees and shrubs waving in the shadows. After a moment someone speculated that it was probably one of the Castle officials but the witness refuted this saying the figure she had seen was wearing *'the most outlandish costume.'*

Clearly jittered, the mood suddenly became more sober and the party pressed on along the white gravel path towards the Castle. Very shortly afterwards someone else cried out that they too had seen the figure. They described it as *'a tall man with a very white horrid face'* but what was most noticeable was that *'his eyes burned with hate.'*

Again the party halted but as before, the figure had vanished. By now all eyes were strained in all directions but no one could see it. The breathless party were growing frantic as they hastened towards the Castle. For a while nothing happened but then as they got within a short distance of the Castle walls, someone uttered an exclamation which made them all turn around and they saw hurrying toward them the tall figure of a man wearing a very broad-brimmed black hat, a dark loose flowing cloak and knee breeches.

The two people immediately recognised him as the person they had seen hiding in the trees. At this point they formed the opinion that he was an eccentric foreigner living in the Castle as he was clearly making his way back in the same direction. In true English upper-class style, not wishing to seem rude or improper, they turned round and continued to walk back to the Castle at a slower pace, expecting the stranger to speedily overtake them.

To their surprise however, he did not. But just as they arrived at the Castle entrance, someone noticed that Mrs Manning was no longer with them. When they looked behind they saw her lifeless body lying full length on the gravel walk a short distance away.

They ran back to her and found that she had fainted. When she recovered her composure she told them that when she saw the face of the tall figure in the cloak she instantly recognised him as the same man she had seen peering up at her bedroom window two days previously.

She told her companions *'I was frightened but at the same I time fascinated, just as I had been fascinated before, and I felt myself constrained by some power I could not resist to linger behind and stare at him. While I was thus occupied it came swiftly up to me and poking its white, evil face forward with a dreadful smile, such as no words can describe, thrust out a long, skinny arm, and before I could draw back touched me on the shoulder. My horror was so great I fainted.'*

There was no sign of the mysterious figure and by now the alarm had been raised in the Castle and despite an extensive search by the guards nothing was found. Mrs Manning was in a hysterical state and although her friends tried to pacify her, she refused to be reassured and she remained convinced that she had been touched by evil and that something dreadful would happen to her.

Tragically she was right. Within a few days of returning to her home in the north of England Mrs Manning died when the boat she was in overturned in the sea and she drowned. Whether this was coincidence or a self-fulfilling prophesy brought on by the trauma of her experience is impossible to say. What is known that all of the party who were with her that night and witnessed the cloaked figure suffered grave misfortune within the year. Two of them died unexpectedly, one went bankrupt and two had what was described at the time as 'serious domestic trouble.'

Whether or not this malign figure was indeed the spirit of a member of the Spanish Inquisition sent to the Catholic court of Mary Tudor in the 1550s is unknown. This was certainly a religiously turbulent period and it is not beyond the realms of possibility that Papal intermediaries were sent to advise Mary as she embarked upon one of the bloodiest chapters of English history, which saw the torture and violent deaths of an estimated 300 Protestant heretics during her short reign.

If the evil spirit of a Spanish Inquisitor still haunts Windsor Castle, it has not been reported for over eighty years or perhaps his victims did not live long enough to tell the tale.

Although elsewhere on the Long Walk towards the Castle, other similar spectral figures have been sighted. In the 1930s a young couple walking through the Park at about 9 o'clock in the evening were caught in a sudden thunderstorm. They ran for cover under a shelter erected in the park for the deer fodder. The girl then realised that just to the side of her was a tall dark figure dressed in a black cloak and wearing a high crowned black hat. She made some polite conversation with him about the weather but he never responded and simply turned his back on her. At that point she and her companion suddenly realised something was not right and felt very afraid. Without uttering a word to each other they fled from their shelter into the storm. When they looked back from a safe distance the man was gone.

Some years later at 11.30 in the morning a not-dissimilar figure was seen by Mrs Hill who was taking her small children for a walk on the Long Walk. About five minutes after they had passed through the gates half-way up the avenue they stopped to rest on the grass. Mrs Hill saw the figure approaching from a distance away. She noticed the distinctive clothing and assumed it was someone on their way to a party at the Castle. She described him as very tall, with a long face and a straight nose and very dark eyes staring out coldly at her. He was wearing a long black cape with the collar turned up and a wide brimmed hat. It was not until he reached a group of grazing deer that she realised he was *'not of this world.'* He glided through them and other than glance in his direction they did not seem alarmed by him. Mrs Hill was terrified and hugged her children close to her chest, rooted to the spot in fear. The spectral figure glided towards them passing within 5 feet before swiftly turning and disappearing into the side of a large tree about 2 yards away.

Mrs. Hill grabbed her children and fled in terror convinced she had witnessed a phantom from an earlier age.

Chapter 6
THE PETRIFYING PORTENT
OF BUCKINGHAM'S MURDER

SIR GEORGE VILLIERS, (1592-1628) was described by one of his contemporaries as the *'handsomest-bodied man in all of England'* and used his charm to inveigle himself into the court of King James I, where he quickly rose to prominence under his Royal patron. He was rewarded for his services to the Crown with the title of 1st Duke of Buckingham, making him the highest-ranking subject in the Kingdom.

He became a much-reviled figure amongst peers and public alike, because of the undue influence he had with the monarch and was strongly suspected to be James' lover. A shrewd courtier, his ambitions were not blunted even after Charles I came to the throne with whom he continued to exploit his privileged position. After demonstrating incompetent military leadership, which necessitated heavy taxation to pay for his mistakes, Parliament attempted twice to impeach the Duke but was always thwarted by the intervention of the King.

Public opinion was so strong against him, that a London mob attacked and killed his physician John Lambe, who was believed to have exerted a diabolical influence over him and the King. Among the pamphlets issued after the murder, one prophesied;

'Let Charles and George do what they can,
The Duke shall die like Doctor Lambe.'

This outpouring of hatred for Buckingham must also have extended to the supernatural realm, as the ghost of his father, also called Sir George Villiers, appeared one night at Windsor Castle to a terrified Keeper of the Royal Robes in an effort to avert his son's murder.

This remarkable ghost story was first told in 1702 by Edward Hyde, The Earl of Clarendon, a trusted and highly credible adviser to Charles I and Charles II, in his book *The History of the Rebellion and Civil Wars in England*.

The story goes that one of the Keepers of the Robes at Windsor Castle, believed to be a certain Mr Towes, had been bought up in his youth at a college in the parish where George Villiers senior was also educated. Although they were close friends at the time, the friendship did not continue after they left. Over thirty years later, seven months before the murder of the Duke, the Keeper was in bed at Windsor when he was visited by a ghost at midnight who drew back the bed curtains and asked if he recognised him. At first he was rigid with fear and unable to reply. The spectre asked again and the Keeper told him he recognised him as George Villiers. The phantom told him he must visit his son, the Duke of Buckingham and warn him;

'...that he must exert himself to make himself popular – otherwise he would not be suffered to live long.'

After he had uttered these words the apparition vanished. The Keeper, after recovering from his terrifying ordeal, finally fell asleep and by the next morning had convinced himself that it had all been a dream and although the impact it had on him was very strong, he tried to put it out of his mind. A night or two later the same ghostly figure appeared as before and asked whether the task had been performed. When the Keeper admitted that it had not, the ghost became even more fearsome and warned him that if he failed to comply, he would haunt him forever. The terrified Keeper promised that he would, and the phantom vanished once more.

By morning he had spent a sleepless night. He now knew that this was not a dream and although he dreaded another visitation, he could not begin to think how he would gain an audience with so grand a figure as the Duke – and even if he could, how he would make him believe he had been visited by his father's ghost. For several days he wrestled with what to do then one night, what he feared most happened again, a third terrifying visitation from the impatient and increasingly terrifying ghost. The Keeper begged to be released from this task explaining that he would not be believed and they would consider him a madman.

The ghost again emphasised that he would have no rest for the rest of his life, until the duty had been done but told him a secret shared by him and the Duke. Once it was related to the Duke, it would immediately convince him that the message was from his father. With that, the supernatural tormentor again disappeared.

The next day the Keeper set off to London to try to arrange a meeting

Sir George Villiers, Duke of Buckingham by Michiel J. van Miereveld.
Wikimedia Commons

with the Duke. He met with Sir Ralph Freeman, the Master of Requests who was married to a relative of the Duke. He implored Sir Ralph, whom he knew well, to gain him a private but urgent audience with the Duke. Seeing his distressed condition, Sir Ralph told him that the Duke would be riding the hunt with the King the next morning from Lambeth Bridge. The two agreed to meet at 5am to see what could be done.

The following morning the Keeper met Sir Ralph and as promised he introduced him to the Duke who arrived by boat. The Duke was very courteous and spoke with him for almost an hour but was unconvinced – until the Keeper disclosed the secret imparted to him by the ghost. The Duke's face changed colour and he flew into a rage telling him that the Devil must have told him this because no-one other than the Duke and one other living person knew of it, and they would tell no-one.

The Duke left the meeting clearly flustered and distracted and continued with the Royal hunt. That afternoon he visited his mother, in her apartments at Whitehall, with whom he spent two or three hours in loud and angry conversation. Witnesses reported he was crimson with rage when he left and she was distraught and in floods of tears. This was highly unusual behaviour, as he held his mother in very high regard and treated her with the utmost respect.

Although she loved her son deeply his mother expressed no surprise at all when a few short weeks later she heard of his assassination. It was evident that he had related the ghostly premonition to her and had accused her of betraying some dark secret, we know not what, which had ended up with the Keeper of the Robes at Windsor Castle.

Buckingham failed to respond to his father's warning from beyond the grave, and as predicted, met with a violent end on 23 August 1628, at the Greyhound Pub in Portsmouth, where he had gone to organise another shambolic military campaign. He was fatally stabbed, but lived just long enough to shout 'Villain!' and chase after his assailant, but then fell down dead. The assassin was Lieutenant John Felton, an army officer who had been wounded in one of Buckingham's failed military expeditions and believed he had been passed over for promotion by him.

Such was the Duke's unpopularity by this time that Felton was widely hailed as a hero by the public, although he was nonetheless hanged for murder the following November.

PART TWO
WINDSOR TOWN

Chapter 7
PANIC AROUND PEASCOD STREET

PEASCOD STREET WHICH runs down from Thames Street and Castle Hill, is one of the oldest streets in Windsor. The name derives from *'Pes croft'* an area where peas were grown, which was a staple food in medieval times. Today it is the main shopping street and despite the modern shop fronts, many of the buildings are very old and harbour supernatural secrets behind their shutters.

At number **6 Peascod Street** is a pair of houses which were originally built in 1866. They have variously been a grocers' shop, a tobacconist and later a bakery. Indeed the oven still exists in the basement. In recent years it has been the home of H. Samuels the Jewellers. An assistant who had worked there for over fifteen years reported that a former colleague, now dead, who had worked there in the 1970s, saw the ghost of a tall man in grey in the shop. An array of ghostly phenomena has been reported at the premises over the years including items in the shop window being moved around, the curtains around the windows being mysteriously drawn when there was no-one in the shop and an uncomfortable presence being reported by those who work there, as if they were being watched by unseen eyes. Many of the staff do not like having to go upstairs to fetch stock. On one occasion one of the female assistants went into the front room which overlooks Peascod Street and whilst she was in there looking through boxes, she clearly heard a man's voice behind her, although she didn't catch what he said. She turned around believing a colleague had followed her upstairs only to find that she was quite alone in the room which had suddenly become icy cold. The assistant flew down the stairs in a state of panic and refused to go to the stockroom again on her own.

Baristas at the **Costa Coffee House** and staff at neighbouring shops have reported similar supernatural activity. Staff working there have reported feeling uncomfortable when alone in the shop as if there was an invisible presence with them. They have reported hearing strange bumps and bangs as though someone is moving around in the premises even when there is no-one

Peascod Street, Windsor c. 1914. ©Royal Windsor Website

else there. To date nothing has been actually seen and the shop staff sincerely hope it remains that way.

At **Elizabethan House** in Peascod Street a sixteenth-century building is now a commercial premises and staff report sudden drops in temperature regardless of the weather. The owners of the shop and their assistants have also heard the sound of ghostly footsteps going upstairs but never coming down.

Around the corner in Thames Street opposite Queen Victoria's statue stands **Ye Harte and Garter** which was built on the site of one of Windsor's oldest coaching inns, The Garter. It was here that Samuel Pepys' diary records that he spent the night on 26 February 1666 when visiting St George's Chapel and Eton College. Legend also has it, that Shakespeare once stayed here and wrote at least part of *The Merry Wives of Windsor* at the inn.

It was once the home of Richard Gallis a former mayor of Windsor and a central figure in the case of the Witches of Windsor which will be discussed later.

During the seventeenth century the inn also housed one of the town's bakeries. On a cold February night in 1629 a fire started in the bakery which quickly gained a hold and destroyed a significant part of the timber-framed building. It was fortunate that it did not spread further down the tightly packed Tudor street but was frightening enough to have the town up in arms. An eight-year-old baker's assistant came under suspicion and was accused of starting the fire. It is not known whether it was deliberate, accidental or even whether he was responsible, but he was tried and convicted for arson and sentenced to death.

Local folklore claims that he was arrested, tried and hanged the same day by the townsfolk, within sight of the charred remains of the inn; however this is not altogether accurate. Research shows that on or about 23 February 1629, one John Dean, described in court documents as *'an infant between eight and nine years,'* was hanged 50 miles away in Abingdon for setting fire to two barns in Windsor.

Justice did however appear to be as swift as legends suggests. *The History of the Pleas of the Crown 1847* confirms that this juvenile felon was indicted, arraigned and found guilty all on the same day, 23 February, *'and was hanged accordingly.'*

The age of criminal responsibility in England at the time was seven years. It was later raised to eight years, and in 1963 to ten years, where it currently remains. Even in the barbaric days of capital punishment, it was unusual for children of this age to be hanged; often their death sentence was commuted to imprisonment. For reasons lost to history, he was not given the usual mercy: even though no-one was killed or even injured in the fire. The contemporary accounts state that the judge found that John Dean had *'malice, revenge, craft and cunning,'* and refused to recommend a reprieve. Perhaps the boy had a prior criminal record or perhaps he was simply a convenient scapegoat in the public uproar which followed the fire. He is said to have been the youngest person ever hanged in England and his tragic death must surely be one of the most shameful episodes in the long and illustrious history of Windsor. His troubled spirit is said to haunt the Harte and Garter to this day and the ghost of a *'ragged young boy'* has been seen by both staff and visitors.

Curfew House, opposite the Curfew Tower, is haunted by the ghost of an old gossip who once lived there and worked at the Castle. She had the unfortunate habit of telling tales on her neighbours and one of them soon decided she had gone too far and would have to be disposed of. He established an alibi by chatting to one of the Castle guards for a little longer than usual, then after the gates were secured for the night, slipped away via the *sally-port*, a secret tunnel used in times of siege. Emerging in the town, he made his way to the old woman's house and viciously threw her over a banister where she plummeted to her death. Although strongly suspected of the crime, the killer's alibi held firm and he was never brought to justice. The restless spirit of the old woman now haunts the house and has cast a malign presence over it. One room was so haunted that the father-in-law of a young couple who lived there, flatly refused to ever spend a night in the house again after enduring a terrible ordeal, the details of which were never disclosed. The atmosphere is described as oppressive and intimidating and visitors have experienced an overwhelming and almost uncontrollable urge to throw themselves over the banisters.

The adjacent houses in **Thames Street** are over 400 years old. One of them, now a shop, was once part of a Tudor inn which housed many guests to the Castle. Shoppers have reported feeling a slight push in the back and have turned around to find no-one is there. The adjacent building was also part of the old inn and was once the home of the Deacon family from 1916 – and an array of ghosts.

Mrs Deacon saw two visions of a figure she believed was Cardinal Wolsey both on Easter Thursday, although two years apart. He appeared in his red robes and Cardinal's hat, wringing his hands and pacing the room with a troubled demeanour. Mrs Deacon wrote:

'It was Easter week about 1921 or 1922. I was not very well so I prepared a meal for the children for when they came home from school and went and lay down in my bedroom which is a very quaint old Tudor room. The room was not darkened as it was a bright spring morning about noon, something drew my attention to the opposite side of the room from where I was lying and to my amazement I saw a figure, perfectly clearly. I knew at once it was Cardinal Wolsey, tall, well-built, attired in the well-known red robe and hat. His face was not as clear as the whole figure but I knew instinctively that it was Cardinal Wolsey. There was no shadow of doubt in my mind which was perfectly clear. He walked very slowly with bowed head as if in deep thought. Slowly he passed right through my bed, through the wall, backwards and forwards, never looking to either side. After pacing thus for about the fourth time the figure slowly dispersed before my eyes.

I had gazed at him earnestly all the time wondering what could be the cause of his appearing in that manner in this room and house, as I had never associated him with the house at any time. I was not a bit frightened, only perfectly mystified. Very soon after my son who was about thirteen or fourteen, came to my room to enquire if there was anything he could get for me. At once I asked him if he knew what became of Cardinal Wolsey when he was sent away from the Castle in disgrace by King Henry VIII. At once he replied "He took refuge in an old inn in the town." Instantly I felt in my mind that this was the old inn.

The second appearance was about two years after this. Everything was the same, a peculiar coincidence, it being Holy Thursday at noon. I was lying quietly resting absolutely normal; the room in the same condition and not darkened when to my intense astonishment there appeared in exactly the same place Cardinal Wolsey only in a black robe and head dress. He was evidently in deep distress wringing his hands together, his head bent down. He seemed old and worn. Without glancing at me or looking anywhere but absolutely straight in front of him, again he passed back- wards and forwards through my massive mahogany bed and walking through the wall, continuing for about four to six times then disap- pearing as mysteriously as he had appeared. The feeling it aroused in me was of pity and sympathy and I never saw him again.'

Mrs Deacon did however have other supernatural experiences at the house. She encountered a mysterious thick black musty-smelling vapour appearing from nowhere in one of the rooms. Several of the family began to complain of terrible night-

Cardinal Wolsey who haunts a former inn in Thames Street. Wellcome Library London

mares of a horrible old man with a withered leg, dragging off the bedclothes and trying to strangle them. They would wake up breathless, bathed in sweat and gasping for breath with the bedclothes rearranged all around them. Mrs Deacon, who clearly had some psychic sensitivity, became convinced the root of the problem lay in the cellar and had it excavated where she was surprised to find evidence of an old chapel dating from many centuries before. Her sons started to dig through the old brick floor only to discover a medieval cooking pot filled with the charred bones of babies. A Catholic priest was called in and said prayers in the cellar. The remains of the bodies were buried in consecrated ground and the pot, it is said, was displayed for many years in the Guildhall Museum. This brought an end to the bad dreams and the mysterious smoke.

Another ghost, who was given the name 'Fred,' was a priest or monk in a brown cowl. He was seen on several occasions seemingly searching for some- thing. He was friendly to the family and caused them no trouble at all. After the departure of the Deacons, the subsequent family were somewhat more nervous. Although they heard strange noises in the house they never investi- gated and avoided using the upper floors of the building for fear what they might see.

Off Thames Street once existed a dark courtyard known as **Cut-Throat Alley**. Its grim name was derived from the local legend that victims of foot- pads which stalked the alleyways of Windsor had been murdered and buried there. The court was finally closed off and became part of a garden belonging to a respectable local citizen named Mr Pond. In the hope of ending local chatter about the murders, he had the garden dug up only to find several skeletons just a couple of feet below ground. Whether or not these were indeed murder victims or relics of an ancient burial was never ascertained.

Could the discovery of a curious corpse over a century ago explain the paranormal activity which has been experienced at **1 Thames Street** over the years? This ancient building was originally an old inn but for over a hundred years was Charles Leyton's Confectionery Shop and had a reputation of being haunted with strange noises being heard and ghostly figures reportedly seen. In 1897 during the extension of the neighbouring Great Western Railway for Victoria's Diamond Jubilee, a lead coffin was discovered. On examination it was found to contain the body of a man wearing a shroud and woollen cap. It was believed to be the body of a Hawaiian Chieftain who had died in the building during a visit to King George III.

During the twentieth century, the premises were occupied by Mr and Mrs Baldrey, the resident managers for the firm of Findlater, Mackie & Todd. One day she was in the upstairs flat alone when she saw a figure of a man in a cap and gown coming towards her who disappeared in an instant. Some months later she awoke in the middle of the night to see a tall well-built man in a straw hat. He said nothing but turned around and went out, closing the bedroom door after him, something she and her husband never did. A few months later the same man again appeared in the bedroom and this time he seemed to smile at Mrs Baldrey and raised his hat. She watched incredulous as he walked to the door, nodded and smiled again. She had the feeling that he was saying his farewells and indeed she never saw him again.

The Baldrey's did however experience other phenomena at the property. They heard ghostly footsteps and their normally placid dog growled and bared his teeth at an invisible presence. These footsteps continued to be heard over the decades by successive occupants and even into the 1980s when it was owned by Itek International. The cleaners heard footsteps and believed them to be early morning burglars but no-one else was found in the building. Members of the office staff reported seeing the apparition of a figure wearing a cap and gown, very similar to the figure seen by Mrs Baldrey decades previously. Other employees described the man as wearing a coachman's cloak with a short cape on top.

Long before the stable of films of the same name, 'paranormal activity' was on the billing at the **Playhouse Cinema** which used to stand in lower Thames Street near the Eton footbridge, opposite Christopher Wren's House. Prior to the demolition of the cinema in the 1970s, many cinema staff saw the ghost of a woman in a long dress who used to materialise on the stage late at night.

The haunted Playhouse Cinema, Thames Street now demolished   Author's Collection

Sudden drops in temperature and the sound of running footsteps were also experienced. Strangely many of the phenomena occurred in mid-February. One former cinema manager admitted he was so terrified when he saw the ghost, that he was physically unable to move through fear.

The cinema was built on the site of a row of eighteenth century houses. One explanation that has been suggested is that the haunting is related to the unsolved murder of a Victorian woman in a bicycle shop which used to stand on the ground floor of one of the Georgian buildings.

The **Theatre Royal** in Thames Street like many other old theatres is haunted by a number of ghosts. In January 2001 during a pantomime production starring John Challis and the late Eric Sykes, the company were startled by cupboard doors flying open of their own accord and pearls mysteriously scattered across the floor as if being thrown by an unseen hand. The audience reportedly resisted the urge to shout 'She's behind you!'

This type of poltergeist activity has been witnessed for over 100 years. The original building, dating from 1823 was destroyed by fire in 1908 and although contemporary accounts do not mention any fatalities, it is widely believed in the town that a nine-year-old girl named Charlotte, perished in the blaze and her ghost now haunts the present theatre, rebuilt on the same site. Charlotte is believed to be in the company of the ghost of a young boy aged around seven years old and the two impish spirits are seen playing hide and seek around the interior of the theatre. There are several isolated storage areas which the staff refuse to visit alone because of the creepy sensation that the mischievous children are lurking in the shadows watching them.

During the autumn of 2014, in preparation for a Halloween-inspired season of ghostly productions, a team from the Berkshire Paranormal Group was invited in to conduct a supernatural assessment. The team, which included psychic mediums and technical experts, encountered a rich seam of paranormal activity.

Down the narrow corridors, psychics reported smelling candle wax and feeling a burning sensation at the spot where a second fire is believed to have started in the theatre when a candle fell from a wall bracket and caused considerable damage.

The ghost of a well-bred, but impatient lady dressed in Victorian clothes, is regularly seen in the fourth row of the upper circle. She has been heard to cry out *'When is the show starting?'* It is believed she is the ghost of a genteel lady called 'Elizabeth' who has benignly haunted the theatre for many years and refuses to leave. During one psychic investigation, two gentlemen of the local press, unaware of the story of Elizabeth, were placed in the row of seats where she is normally seen. Both were reported to have 'freaked out' when they were touched on the shoulder by an invisible hand – perhaps Elizabeth politely trying to ease them out of her seat?

Another ghost is said to haunt changing room number 3 which frequently experiences an ice-cold chill and the smell of fresh flowers. It is said to be home to a phantom actress who was murdered there following a blow on the head from a deranged fan and now can never leave the room.

The theatre management report a recent incident which took place after closing time late one night. The duty manager doing his rounds carefully closed and locked a set of double internal doors. When he returned a short time later, he found that they had inexplicably burst wide open to the walls causing him to flee in terror.

In one part of the theatre lobby, pipe smoke can be frequently smelt, even though smoking is strictly forbidden on the premises, and curiously it cannot be detected just a short distance away.

The final entity may be indicative of a much darker secret. Medium Charlotte Whalley believes that the spirit and the earthly remains of a nineteenth century woman called Mary Ann remain trapped somewhere in the walls of the old theatre. Mary Ann was believed to have lived at the house, which was formerly a private home, on the right hand side of the theatre. Charlotte believes the tragic figure lived with her husband John who killed her and her black Labrador dog after a violent argument. The ghost of Mary Ann and her phantom dog now haunt the building, unable to leave until their bodies are found. Her husband, riddled with guilt is also believed to haunt the theatre which has since been expanded to incorporate their former home. In life he escaped justice and in death he is sentenced to roam the earth as a restless spirit.

Just around the corner, the former **Travers College** in Datchet Road dates from 1803 when it was founded as a home for poor and distressed naval officers known as Naval Knights. The charitable scheme was abandoned in 1892 and the last three Naval Knights were reluctant to leave and resign their pensions. Remaining defiant until the end, Governor Wallis, had to be forcibly ejected from the building on 20 January 1893 and it is believed that he returned to haunt the building after his death. The college was subsequently converted to a boy's school for the choristers of St George's Chapel.

In the 1920s a motorist driving home late along **Datchet Road** from London to Windsor had to brake suddenly when a phantom coach and horses crossed his path. He described it as *'a stagecoach of the oldest pattern'* which passed slowly across the road and through a fence on the opposite side into a field. When newspaper reports circulated of the incident, a number of other people came forward to say they too had witnessed the same phenomenon along this stretch of road.

The Old House Hotel now known as **Sir Christopher Wren's House** is a wonderful riverside hotel occupying a prime position across the Thames from Eton. Although Christopher Wren lived in Windsor when his father became Dean of St George's Chapel, there is no proof that there was any direct link between this building and the great man, but it is certainly a fine example of Grade II listed Georgian architecture.

It has had a reputation as a haunted house for centuries. Records show that in 1788 the house was owned by the Jervoise family who had taken it to be close to their son who attended Eton College.

It was later the residence of the Cheshire family and was a very lively home, full of society and hospitality, until his youngest daughter became pregnant out of wedlock. Such was the shame and social stigma in the early nineteenth century that Mr. Cheshire confined her to her bedroom at the back of the house and her only experience of the outside world was being allowed to walk in the walled garden away from public gaze. Tragically the illegitimate child died in childbirth and it is after this that the fortunes of the Cheshire family took a sudden turn for the worse, and led to the speculation that the house was cursed.

Several members of the family were struck down by tropical diseases despite never having visited the tropics. Mr Cheshire almost died from food poisoning and although his health recovered, his finances collapsed and he was forced the sell the house and move into a smaller property.

When his elder daughter became engaged to a peer, Lord Fauconberg, he believed he had at last broken the curse but according to some sources the bride was jilted at the last minute because of Mr Cheshire's financial problems. In fact the wedding did take place but the groom tragically died soon afterwards from a fit of apoplexy. All of this added to the mythology of the curse and strengthened the rumour that the house was haunted. A succession of owners came and went during the subsequent 100 years many of whom reported seeing the mournful ghost of a young woman wandering aimlessly around the walled garden.

In the latter part of the nineteenth century, the house was taken by Baroness de Vaux. Her son was much amused by a ghost in one of the smaller bedrooms up the back staircase, which is believed to be the one where Miss Cheshire had been confined. His mother refused to sleep in that room because of its eerie atmosphere. She found it impossible to retain staff at the house, and servants left in droves claiming to have seen ghostly figures. Around 1918, the house was left empty for some years and its derelict and foreboding appearance, together with its false windows, led it to acquire the ominous local nickname of *'The Haunted House'*.

Many people were so intimidated by it that they took a detour rather than walk past it, for fear of seeing a ghostly face peering out at them from the grimy windows. However in the 1920s two plucky sisters, the Misses Outlaw, bought the house convinced it was haunted, and ran it successfully for many years as the Riverholme Restaurant and Guest House.

Mrs Olive Eccles and her husband stayed as guests in the room in the1970s. One night they returned to the hotel at about 12.45 am after spending the evening with some friends. They went straight to bed and fell asleep almost immediately. Mrs Eccles awoke a little time later to find a man standing in the darkened room next to a chest of drawers. At first she though it was her husband but then noticed he was asleep beside her. She then feared it might be an intruder and so kept very still to avoid possible attack and continued to watch him, intending to raise the alarm when he left the room. The figure loomed silently towards the bed and approached the closed bathroom door. When it reached the door it vanished. Mrs Eccles who swears she was wide awake at the time felt nothing frightening or menacing about the figure.

Today the house is owned by a major hotel chain and seems to have shaken off its paranormal past. At least any nocturnal supernatural activity which may have taken place, has not yet made its way onto the pages of Trip Advisor.

Chapter 8
HAUNTINGS AROUND HIGH STREET

MARKET CROSS HOUSE must surely be one of the quaintest buildings in Windsor. The original Market Cross House was built in 1592 and stood at the crossroads where Castle Hill meets the High Street. It served the town for less than a century before it was demolished along with many other medieval buildings to make way for new development. In 1687 the Guildhall was being extended by Sir Christopher Wren and it was ordered by town officials that the Market Cross House should be re-built at the same time. It was hastily constructed uncomfortably in the space between the Guildhall and Queen Charlotte Street, which, at 51 feet 10 inches (15.8m) long is reputed to be the shortest street in Britain. The house was built using a framework of unseasoned green oak which twisted over the years and has led to its characteristic crooked appearance and its local nickname of *'The Crooked House'*.

During its long history Market Cross House has had many incarnations including butcher's shop, brewery, grocers, silversmiths, antique shop and a gift shop. It was a popular tea room for many years until recently. The house has a tunnel leading to Windsor Castle which was originally used to transport goods and provisions underground to the Castle. Local legend has it that this was most popularly used in times of poor harvests when food was secretly smuggled through the tunnels to feed the Royal Household, rather than through the open streets which might have incited the starving townsfolk to riot.

For decades, supernatural activity has been associated with the house. In December 1997 a woman visiting from overseas, unfamiliar with the history of the house, entered the tea-room and stopped dead in her tracks. She announced to the staff, *'You have a female ghost don't you?'* Wendy Baynes who was working there at the time, was somewhat taken aback and answered hesitantly *'Yes – we do have a ghost but we always thought it was a man. How did you know?'*

The customer, who was clearly psychically gifted, lifted her arm and pointed at the wall and said, *'When I came in I saw the figure of a woman standing there leaning over a fireplace rubbing her hands together as if warming herself in front of a coal fire.'*

The visitor went on to describe in some details the figure she had seen. *'She was an old lady with grey hair in a bun with a long skirt and a high-collared blouse.*

Market Cross House, Windsor High Street haunted by an Edwardian lady
Wikimedia Commons

As I looked at her she seemed to be aware of me looking and then turned slowly towards me and smiled before slowly disappearing.'

Wendy recalled: *'The hairs on my neck stood on end because this confirmed all the experiences we had had over the years in the shop. The only thing which didn't make sense at the time was the fireplace because as far as we knew, where the customer had seen the ghost, was just a cupboard which we used to store crockery. Then some months later we had to have some work done in the shop which uncovered a bricked-up fireplace behind the cupboard exactly where she had seen the woman warming her hands.'*

It is difficult to understand how the customer could possibly have known there was a fireplace at that location in the shop, it is not evident and even those who had worked there for many years had no idea of its existence.

Wendy and her daughter Kerry went on to describe a catalogue of mysterious events which perplexed and spooked the staff who worked there.

'There have been many small things like a sink plug which mysteriously disappeared off its chain one day and was never seen again. We used to blame the ghost which we called "Harry" for being mischievous. We were convinced he used to steal spoons as we lost them by the dozen. We tried to pacify him but the activity got worse and worse and for over a year we lost count of the number of strange incidents we had, including several electrical malfunctions of brand new industrial equipment. We had cafetieres and crockery jump off shelves and smash on the floor even though there was no-one anywhere near them.'

There were two incidents which particularly scared Kerry and Wendy. *'One night before locking up we arranged the tables for the next morning and placed a little posy of artificial flowers on each of the tables. When we opened up the next morning, every one of them had gone – we couldn't believe it as no-one else had access to the premises.'*

On a different morning the owners opened up to find that the whole café was in disarray. *'Our first though was that we had been burgled but there was no sign of a forced entry. There was tea spilt all over the floor, crockery smashed and creepiest of all, the teapots were intertwined with spouts threaded through the handles, even though they had been placed neatly on a shelf the evening before.'*

After the 'psychic' customer told them their phantom was a woman, they took to calling her 'Ella' and thereafter the mischievous or disapproving poltergeist activity all but ceased, apart from the occasional item being moved. Wendy believes the ghost was a former owner of the house from late Victorian times and perhaps objected to being referred to as a man and was making her displeasure known.

Her presence was felt right up until the tearoom closed, particularly in one room on the second floor which was used as an office and contained the staff toilets. This had a constant icy chill regardless of the weather outside and visits to 'spend a penny' were always made very quickly to avoid being in the room for any longer than necessary. It remains to be seen what 'Ella' will make of her next earthly lodgers.

Opposite Market Cross house is **24 High Street**, currently occupied by fashion store Cath Kidston where a ghostly presence has been reported haunting the store room which makes staff nervous to be in the premises alone.

Castle Hill House opposite King Henry VIII gate on Castle Hill, was for many years used as nurse's accommodation. The present building was built between 1746 and 1788, on the site of the ominously named 'The *Sign of the Devil'* tavern. Several unearthly incidents have been reported during its long history. It is currently home to the Inigo Business Centre where several workers have reported feeling uneasy in the house when alone, and sudden inexplicable drops in temperature have been experienced.

Even as late as 2010 staff reported mysterious activity in the basement and believe it to be the spirit of a maid who used to work there. Visiting clients have expressed a feeling of anxiety when entering the basement and cleaners

were very nervous about visiting this area of the building, particularly after hours when there was no-one else around. The building is now unoccupied during the hours of darkness and so no nocturnal phenomena have been reported for some years.

The Drury House in Church Street is popularly, but inaccurately, known as *'Nell Gwynn's House'* and is said to be haunted by her ghost. It was built in the reign of King Charles I, in 1645, originally to house the staff from Windsor Castle. It was then rumoured to be part of the abode of Nell Gwynn, Charles II's favourite Mistress, to accommodate their secret liaisons. Local legend claims a tunnel was built between the Drury House and the Castle, enabling Nell Gwynn to have a secret romantic rendezvous with the King at short notice. Although the tunnel does exist, it pre-dates Nell

Church Street Windsor showing Nell Gwynn's house and Henry VIII Gate by E.W. Haslehust 1910. Wikimedia Commons

Gwynn by several centuries and was used in the event of the Castle being besieged to smuggle provisions in and out. The tunnel is still in existence to this day, though for security reasons, has been partially blocked off.

Furthermore Nell Gwynn never actually lived in the house. At that time the street was called Fish Street and it was a very smelly place indeed being filled with fishmonger's shops and butchers all of whom tipped their waste and offal out onto the cobbles. Nell Gwynn wisely preferred the more sumptuous surrounding of the Royal Mews round the corner, although it is said she was happy for her maids to live there!

A century later the house was divided up to create separate houses for the employees of the Castle. It then became a utility house, housing coffins, suits of armour and supplies for the Castle before becoming a residential town house in the late eighteenth century. Although Drury House may or may not house the ghost of the flamboyant Nell Gwynn, it does have two other ghosts, one is an undertaker who is seen in the dining area on the second floor and the other is a young girl who plays on the stairs. Murray Northwood from the Berkshire Paranormal Group reported that many people experience a ghostly chill in the room and he has had people who are so troubled by the presence on the second floor, that they have refused to enter the room.

The Drury House is now is now a cosy restaurant owned and run by Steve Turner and his family all of whom have personal experience of mysterious happenings since taking over the business in 2013. Steve explained:

'There's a mirror that distorts reflections even though it never moves, chairs that are left tucked under tables but are pulled out in the morning, and two of the girls who work here have been tripped on the stairs when they were alone.

Two weeks after I moved in, the head chef and I were the only ones left in the building and we were sitting on the ground floor when we suddenly heard a noise from the dumb waiter [a pulley system used to send trays of food up from the kitchen to the dining rooms above]. I went over and found two 50p coins on the floor – earlier in the day I had seen them on the second floor. I tried to dismiss it and not get worked up about it, but as I walked up the stairs I found the two coins back on the second floor again – I dashed into my flat, locked the door and slept with the light on!'

Nearby the ghostly figure wearing *'a stiff white collar and a hat like a Quaker with long flowing hair and a beard'* haunts the former **Engine House Restaurant** at 4 Church Lane (now known as Cody's). The figure was seen clearly in the 1980s by a woman who worked at the restaurant before it vanished right in front of her. Other staff reported hearing phantom footsteps upstairs and the sound of someone moving about. The manageress reported the disturbing experience of finding large male footprints in the bath one morning even though no men lived or worked there at the time.

The tiny '**Anne Page's Cottage**,' tucked behind the High Street, was thought to be haunted by a number of spirits during the Second World War when it was occupied by Mrs Tapley and her daughter. Rustling skirts were heard in the panelled sitting-room and of the two other ghosts; one was hostile and unwelcoming and the other which haunted the upstairs of the building was friendly.

In February 1929 the ghostly apparition of a Beefeater made front page news although surprisingly it was not seen at Windsor Castle but at **The New Inn** in High Street, then one of the town's oldest hostelries which was empty and close to dereliction. The ghost was seen through the large windows on several occasions after midnight woefully roaming the empty rooms of the old inn. The pub was used as accommodation for the Yeoman Warders during the Garter ceremonies during the reign of Queen Victoria and the licensees habitually laid on a spread after the event which was much anticipated and enjoyed by one and all. The lonely Yeoman was remarked to have a sad and lonely expression and wandered around the building aimlessly as if looking for long-gone colleagues.

After one sighting a witness reported;

'I should not have paid a great deal of attention perhaps in the ordinary way, but as I stared I noticed that I could see part of the wall of the room showing through the figure at the window. Suddenly the Yeoman raised his hand as though to salute someone inside the room, and then the apparition vanished.'

A further newspaper report in 1932 after another spate of sightings, bizarrely asserted that the ghost had a grudge against Oliver Cromwell who it was claimed had once stayed at nearby Park Street. On this occasion, the ghost was reported to have been making strange gurgling noises and clapping its hands as though greatly joyous. Its eyes were described as little points of fire which increased in intensity as Christmas Eve drew nigh then as midnight chimed, the eerie intruder grew in luminosity until it vanished completely at the last stroke of twelve. The rather odd phantom Yeoman has not been seen since modern offices replaced the old inn.

Chapter 9
THE WINDSOR 'VAMPIRE'

THE CASE OF the Windsor 'Vampire' is one of the most overlooked and disturbing cases to have ever taken place in the town.

The depraved and bestial activities of Benjamin Spong caused outrage in Georgian Windsor and there is little doubt that had his activities been carried out a century previously, he would have been burnt at the stake for witchcraft.

Benjamin Spong was born in Sunninghill in 1756 and little is known of his early life although at some stage he was employed as a labourer, living and working at 'Woodside' on Crimp Hill, Old Windsor, the manor house now occupied by pop star Sir Elton John. Spong gained a reputation as the 'Woodside Monster' at the end of the eighteenth century for the unspeakable practise of eating live cats. This was not an isolated atrocity and Spong became infamous for prowling the cobbled streets of Windsor in search of his feline prey. In one public demonstration of his horrific predilection in January 1790, he ate a live cat in front of a packed bar at the Prince of Wales pub in Church Street, Windsor and was thrown out by the publican William Watmore. Although disturbingly horrific, Spong committed no criminal offence in doing so, and revelled in his gruesome notoriety committing ever-more unspeakable acts of barbarity.

The following month he demonstrated there were no limits to his grotesque appetite when he publicly hacked off his own hand with a bill hook *'in order to taste living flesh.'* He was prevented from eating it by the intervention of a passing surgeon who found Spong's hand *'severed at the wrist, save for a piece of connecting skin.'*

Despite having only one hand, Spong's reputation grew as a fearsome and dangerous individual whose depravity knew no bounds. One morning in April 1796, his neighbour Mrs Clarke from Old Windsor Green had offered to wash his cravats and Spong went to her house to wait for them. Whilst Spong was waiting for her to finish, he asked if he could take her six-month-old baby son for a walk. Whether or not she had any choice in the matter is not known, but Spong carried the baby away in his arms. Mrs Clarke was doubtless relieved when he returned a short while later saying the baby was sleeping, and so he had put him to bed. Mrs Clarke continued with her laundry and by the afternoon remarked that it was unusual that the child had not started crying by now, as he had slept for most of the day and he would be awake all night if he was not woken.

Spong who was still at the house offered to go and check on the child. He returned shortly afterwards saying that he had bad news, then calmly announced: *'Do not be alarmed but your baby is dead!'*

Dr Woollast was summoned from the town and confirmed to a distraught Mr and Mrs Clarke, that their baby was indeed dead. What shocked them even more was the doctor's revelation that death was due to strangulation.

When the child was undressed, a number of horrific injuries became apparent revealing the infant had been subjected to considerable violence. Besides the heavy bruising around the baby's throat, the skin had been ripped away from the chin, his right femur was broken and the flesh was hanging from his left thigh. There were several large bite marks on the child's torso. Spong had clearly strangled and tried to eat the child and then changed his mind and returned him back to his bed as if nothing had happened.

At the inquest the next day, the Coroner brought in a verdict of wilful murder against Benjamin Spong.

Upon his arrest, Spong denied all knowledge of the child's injuries and claimed that he was not capable of inflicting such injuries in his disabled state. He alleged the child was alive and well when he placed him in the bed. The implication was that someone else was responsible for the child's death and the only other people to have access at the time were his parents. His courtroom performance clearly had the desired effect of raising reasonable doubt within the minds of the jury. Despite strong circumstantial evidence and Spong's known blood-lust and depravity, to the shock of the parents, press and public, he was acquitted of murder at Reading Assizes and released.

Many speculated that the beast must have used witchcraft and dark arts to escape conviction for this inhuman atrocity. In an age when life was cheap and justice was quick and brutal, it was unusual for a suspected murderer to escape the hangman's noose in the face of such evidence, but escape he did.

From the escalating pattern of his monstrous activities, it is difficult to imagine that Spong did not continue with further similar carnage. Although branded as a cannibal and a vampire, he brazenly continued to publicly devour live cats. There are no surviving records of any further barbarous acts against humans, although children routinely went missing during this period and their fate never discovered, often presumed lost in the nearby river Thames. Is it possible that he finally satiated his bestial ambition to eat a child and was never caught?

He was again arrested in 1799 for the larceny of a pair of flannel drawers for which he was *'whipped at the cart's tail'* and imprisoned for twelve months. It did not go unnoticed by the townsfolk of Windsor that a pair of pantaloons was evidently worth more than the life of an infant.

Any further diabolical deeds that he may have been responsible for remained undetected. He lived out the rest of his life in Old Windsor as a figure to be feared and avoided at all costs. He died in 1824 at the age of sixty-eight years and was buried in an unmarked grave at the parish churchyard of St Peter and St Andrew near to the grave of the child whose life he had undoubtedly taken in his monstrous craving for human flesh.

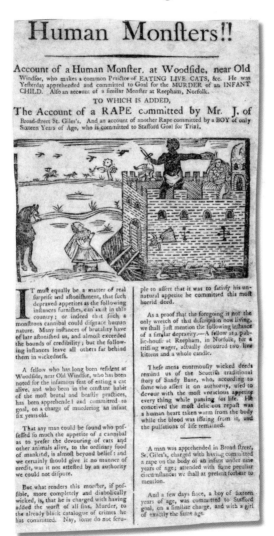

Benjamin Spong the Windsor 'Vampire' who lived at Woodside, the house now owned by Sir Elton John.
Wikimedia Commons

Chapter 10
PERILOUS PARK STREET

ONE OF THE LESSER-known mysteries of Windsor involves the disconcerting tale of two young boys, William Fenwick aged eleven and his friend William Butterworth aged thirteen and their encounter with a diabolical coachman in 1856.

According to one account the two boys were offered a lift by a stranger driving an unusual horse and carriage known as a 'basket-chaise'. He took them to Albany Road, near Park Street, Windsor where they became drowsy and passed out for no apparent reason. They woke up several hours later in the Home Park in the shadow of Windsor Castle with no recollection of how they got there. In a bizarre post-script a stone head was excavated in Park Street, Windsor in the 1930s. A photograph was shown to William Fenwick who was by now a very old man. He immediately recognised it at the face of the man who had driven the carriage.

It would be easy to dismiss this report as the product of overactive youthful imagination but a little detective work has shown there is a significant element of truth to this strange tale.

In fact the story begins at 6pm on Tuesday 12 September 1856 when the two boys arrived in a disorientated state at the home of Mr Joseph Lundy at the British Schoolhouse, New Road, Windsor. Mr Lundy immediately recognised the elder boy, William Butterworth as a former pupil whom he had not seen for some time after he had moved with his family from Windsor to London. The story that the boys related, concerned him so much that he at once took them to Windsor police station and handed them into the protective custody of the local police chief Superintendent Frederick Eagar.

Superintendent Eagar found the boys to be intelligent and respectably dressed and gave an articulate account of what had befallen them. William Butterworth explained that his father was a trooper in the 2nd Life Guards who had been stationed at Windsor until he died two years previously when he and his mother had moved to 24 Great Edward Street, Regent's Park. William Fenwick, his friend, lived nearby at 38 Edward Street, Regent's Park with his father who was a clerk in the city.

Superintendent Eagar was known to be a shrewd Irishman not easily swayed by a yarn but clearly believed their account, publicly stating that:

'From the simple and artless manner in which they told their extraordinary

tale, there is no reason for suspecting it to be otherwise than true.'

Perhaps the evidence is best imparted in William Fenwick's own words;

'We were standing near the Crown & Anchor at the corner of Edward Street at ten o'clock yesterday morning, when a gentleman drove up in a basket-chaise, and asked Butterworth to hold his horse, which he did for about five minutes. When the gentleman returned, he felt in his pocket and said he had no change, but if we would ride with him to New Road [Windsor], where he lived, he would give us a shilling between us. On arriving at the top of Albany Road, the gentleman gave us something to drink out of a half-pint bottle, which we observed was sealed and tied with a string. The liquid tasted like bitter ale, but was the colour of porter. In about five minutes we were sleepy, and fell asleep immediately afterwards. We remembered nothing else until we found ourselves at half-past five o'clock in the afternoon in the Home Park, close to the river, and within twenty yards of the keeper's house at Victoria-bridge. Butterworth awoke first; he immediately knew where he was, from his having been previously quartered with his father at Windsor. Both our heads ached very much on awaking.'

The boys both gave very detailed descriptions of their abductor which corroborated each other and tended to support their truthfulness.

'The gentleman wore a black coat, black trousers, and a light coloured waistcoat; he was a dark man, about 40, with large black whiskers and moustache. It was a four- wheel low caned vehicle, the hind wheels much larger than those in front. It was a bay horse, with a black tail.'

Nowadays this disturbing incident would have warranted a major investigation. The motives of their abductor can only be speculated upon, but his actions were clearly of a predatory and sinister nature. Despite an extensive man hunt, the mysterious kidnapper was never traced. The boys were however reunited with their distraught parents and thankfully no serious harm was sustained.

The story was long-forgotten by the 1930s when the vicarage of the Windsor parish church of St John the Baptist was moved from the High Street to nearby Park Street. During the building work a strange object was unearthed in the old vicarage garden. It was a carved stone head of something not quite human. It had the face of a man including a large moustache and fierce deep set eyes but had the

Park Street c. 1900 – the home of several Windsor spectres.
© The Royal Windsor Website

ears and antlers of a stag. It became the subject of much local speculation and there were many theories as to its origin. It may have been part of a gargoyle or some other grotesque church ornament, and indeed it has been described as looking something like the carved stone 'Green Man' faces which decorate many churches. Some suggested that it had belonged to William Evingdon the last Keeper of Windsor Great Park, and that it was passed on from Keeper to Keeper as some kind of tradition or symbol of office. It was a matter of historical record that Evingdon had donated the building to the Parish of Windsor in 1487 'for the good of his soul.'

The bizarre stone head became known as the 'Mask of Herne' and William Fenwick who was by now almost ninety years of age was shown a photograph of it and positively identified it as his kidnapper from almost eighty years previously. The credibility of this unconventional identity parade was dubious to say the least, and perhaps this was an example of a newspaper attempting to put a supernatural spin on what was a very earthly abduction. The bewhiskered stone head had a passing resemblance to most of the middle-aged male population of the early Victorian age.

The Mask of Herne unearthed in Park Street and recognised by William Fenwick as his fiendish abductor eighty years later.

Courtesy Michael Bayley

Regrettably the mysterious stone 'Mask of Herne'disappeared in 1963. It had been owned by Mr Bayley until the church reclaimed it in the late 1930s when it was displayed in the garden of the new vicarage in Park Street. It remained there throughout the Second World War until the house was sold and passed into private hands and then placed in the church museum from where it was stolen. Surprisingly given its celebrity at the time, there appear to be no surviving photographs of the figure, merely a tantalisingly crude sketch made by Michael Bayley the son of the man who owned it in the 1930s.

Perhaps somewhere in a dark corner of England, the ancient stone carving now takes pride of place on the mantelpiece of a Druid or is the centrepiece of secret pagan shrine. But whether it actually represents the image of the 'Basket-Chaise Fiend' who so traumatised two Victorian schoolboys is much less likely.

Park Street also has other stories to tell. Gate House near **Black Horse Yard** in Park Street was for many years the home of Miss Smith and her aunt and they firmly believed in the story that the house was haunted, but manifestations only occurred before the death of the reigning monarch. Miss Smith wrote;

> 'Just before the death of Edward VII both my aunt and her aunt and two maids heard a great deal of noise from the cellar like furniture being moved about. They all spoke to each other about it and said they could not sleep well because of it and then the papers announced the sudden illness of the King.'

Black Horse Yard was the stable yard used by King Charles II's physician Sir Charles Scarburgh. Clinking harnesses are said to be heard there and the ghost of the surgeon's carriage is seen thundering out of the yard up towards the Royal Mews on the eve of the death of a monarch. Sir Charles attended to the Merry Monarch during his final illness in February 1685 but the brutal treatment of excessive blood-letting, caustic emetics and poison enemas probably contributed to his slow and painful death rather than doing anything to relieve it.

At around midnight on 6 May 1910 when King Edward VII died, a ghostly carriage drawn by four spectral steeds was seen leaving the yard but never arrived at the Mews. Perhaps it is guilt which drives the phantom physician to appear on these macabre occasions, although why he should appear at Windsor when the King died at Whitehall Palace will have to remain a mystery.

Anne Groom's House in Park Street is situated close to the gates of leading to the Long Walk. Anne killed herself in 1891 after suffering abuse at the hands of her lover. She hanged herself from one of the bedroom windows on the top floor. Since then her spirit has refused to leave the house and her presence is marked by an ice cold spot right outside the front door. Witnesses have experienced a feeling of sadness and depression when approaching the house and some people have found themselves bursting into tears without explanation.

A large and ancient house in the town centre towards the Great Park, named **Maidlea Cottage**, has a very hostile and foreboding atmosphere. In the 1970s it was owned by Mr and Mrs Wakefield-Smith who reported that the ghost of a tall man in a dark cloak was seen by some house guests. The couple also heard the sounds of a frenzied battle and the clash of weapons on armour one evening whilst they were in their garden. This was believed to be the supernatural echo of an ancient skirmish between Britons and Romans which took place in the area.

In the years before the Second World War, Colonel and Mrs Philip Eliot brought up their family in the elegant eighteenth-century **'Anne Foord's House'** in Park Street which is haunted by a number of ghosts including a monk who has woken up the lady of the house on several occasions by walking across the bedroom. On the first occasion she assumed it was her husband and sat up calling out 'Is *that you dear?*' only to find her husband was still asleep next to her and heard the footsteps continue across the floor.

Mrs Eliot heard them many times and whenever she did she sat up and switched the light on but never saw anyone, although the footsteps continued diagonally across the room from an alcove beside the bed to the far wall where they stopped. Mrs Eliot believed the alcove was originally a doorway. She was never frightened of the footsteps and when her husband was away, she slept alone and frequently heard the footsteps while she was wide awake and reading with the light on.

The phantom friar was heard to descend the staircase and the figure of a monk was once seen by the children and their nurse. One of the children recognised him as *'the nice old man who comes in to say goodnight.'* When asked by his mother to describe him, her three year old son said, *'He's like Father Christmas – only wearing burnt paper.'* Perhaps this was a reference to his hooded appearance and his black coarse-textured habit. Mrs Eliot never saw anything but believed *'Thomas'* as she nicknamed him, was the ghost of a monk, from a time when a religious building stood on the site of the house.

One day the Colonel was showing an old gun to a friend who obviously had some psychic ability. He was amazed when instead of paying attention to the gun, the friend declared that he could see a misty figure with a *'sort of white handkerchief'* over its head and neck standing beside the Colonel. It was not until some years later that it was discovered the gun was the type used by the Foreign Legion.

The Eliot's rented out Anne Foord's House in the late 1930s and local author Angus Macnaghten, lived there as a child with his mother for three years before the Second World War and described in his book *Haunted Berkshire*, the unnerving feeling they experienced of being watched by an unseen presence. Although they never saw *'Thomas'* or the ghostly Legionnaire, they were frequently reminded of a presence. The Macnaghten family used to hear the sound of large objects being moved about on the top floor even though it was empty and heard the sound of a little tinkling bell early in the morning as if to herald morning prayers

Chapter 11
SHIVERS AROUND SHEET STREET

SHEET STREET IS rich with supernatural activity, presumably a legacy of the diversity of very old buildings which are located here. Its name is thought to derive from the Anglo Saxon word *'Sceat'* which was piece of cloth used to shroud the dead.

One of the finest houses in the town, **Hadleigh House** sits at the junction with Sheet Street and Victoria Street. It was built in 1793 by the then Mayor of Windsor, William Thomas and in 1811 became the home of John O'Reilly, the apothecary-surgeon to George III.

For many years it was also lived in by Angus Macnaghten who wrote several books on Berkshire ghosts in the 1970s. His mother, who was clearly sensitive to such happenings, witnessed several supernatural phenomena during the twenty-five years the family were resident there.

Footsteps heard on the stairs were commonplace in the house as was unexplained knocking and banging coming from various rooms in the house. On one occasion the drawing-room door was mysteriously, but firmly bolted from the inside, and the sealed room had to be broken into with some difficulty by a locksmith.

Séances were conducted there over the years and on one winter's night whilst Angus and his mother were eating supper, loud knockings started all around the room. They stopped talking and the room was filled with the unmistakable scent of clove carnations, although there were none in the house. The phenomenon lasted about a minute before disappearing.

Interestingly this phenomenon was repeated about fifteen years later, after the Macnaghtens had sold the house to Mrs A. The new owner had redecorated the house after moving in, and had spent the morning, with her daily help Mary, moving furniture into an empty first floor bedroom which had been entirely re-papered and the floor sanded. The two ladies were carrying something into the room when Mary, exclaimed *'What a beautiful smell.'* Mrs A couldn't smell a thing but Mary put down her load and began walking round the room sniffing saying *'You must be able to smell it. It's so strong. It's carnations with a whiff of clove!'* Although Mrs A. was unable to smell the ghostly fragrance then or on any subsequent occasion, she took it as a welcoming omen and lived undisturbed in her happy home for many years.

Not far from Hadleigh House a remarkable apparition was seen by retired detective Frederick Bentley on a piece of land he cultivated on the site of the former grounds of **Abbey House**, which was demolished to make was for the council offices of the Royal Borough of Windsor & Maidenhead. One Sunday evening he had been mowing his lawn when he had a feeling that he was being watched. He recalled:

'I had my back to the area which had previously been Abbey House and its grounds. Some fifteen or twenty yards away I could vaguely see a number of figures. They were indistinct and what I could see of their clothing, was mainly long cloaks or gowns, but one thing was reasonably distinct and significant – the figure on the extreme right of the line was wearing a tall hat with a wide brim and a white sort of collar of unusual size. I just stood and stared but had no urge to investigate, it was a warm night but I suddenly felt chilled. Later that night I realised where I had seen such a tall hat and wide collar – this was the traditional dress of the Puritans of Cromwell's England.'

Mr Bentley had other ghostly experiences at his home which was the top floor flat at **Old Institute House**, an eighteenth-century house in Sheet Street. Frequently on call as part of the CID, Mr Bentley would often be returning home during the early hours of the morning. He often found that on reaching the first floor landing there was a strange and inexplicable drop in temperature. Other visitors had also commented on this, and the general eeriness of the building.

However during one evening he had an unnatural experience whilst alone in his flat that he would never forget. As was his usual habit, Mr Bentley had been reading in bed before switching off his bedside lamp. There was a bay window on the south side overlooking a flat roof and a small leaded window pane on the east side facing the garden. He suddenly became conscious that he was not alone in the room. He sat up and saw a figure at the end of his bed.

In his own words he describes it as follows: *'He could not have been more than five feet six inches in height, was beautifully proportioned and may well have been stark naked! I was sitting in bed, I was unable to see his lower limbs but his head arms and torso were perfectly visible. He was standing at a slight angle which permitted the moon partially to illuminate his body. In the shock of seeing the figure my immediate reaction was to shout out. "What the hell do you think you're doing?" As I said it, I rolled sideways and switched on the bedside lamp. The room was flooded with light but the intruder had gone.'*

Mr Bentley searched the room but it was obvious that no-one was in the room and no-one could have left. He realised then that he had seen a ghost. Mr Bentley described him in some detail as:

'A native of some kind, possibly a Polynesian, for his skin was lighter than most coloured men and his hair which was thick and crinkly was rather short but appeared rounded as if indicative of the shape of his head. His body glistened

and gave me the impression that it was coated with an oil of some description. But it was his eyes! His eyes were extremely large and wide open, the whites seeming to increase the size of them. He just stood there staring at me, his expression seeming to be one of curiosity. There was nothing menacing about him or his attitude. Only after I had switched on the light and completed my search of the room, did I begin to feel a little uneasy. If you have seen a dog's hackles rise as it confronts another dog and prepares to fight, this is precisely what I felt. I could actually feel the hair standing on the back of my neck.'

What Mr Bentley saw that night remains a mystery but remained with him for the rest of his days. He later suggested this bizarre nocturnal visitor may have seen a former patient from a leper colony or an inmate of the Pest House; this is unlikely as the leper colony was housed at Spital not in Sheet Street and the Old Pest House was on the opposite side of the road although it too has at least one ghost of its own.

Sheet Street was the home of an old plague pit where the bodies of plague victims were buried when the disease ravaged Windsor in the seventeenth century. **The Old Pest House** or hospital itself was situated at 29 Sheet Street. The three storey house was formerly the workhouse and a town gaol but more recently it was the home of John and Margaret Mills who ran it as a small hotel. It was haunted by the spirit of a very thin old man whom the family nicknamed *'George'*. He wore a dark cloak and appeared most often ascending the stairs where the family often sensed his presence and moved aside to let him pass. Dogs too were aware of him but unusually greeted him with a wagging tail.

Curiously it was noticed that he became more visible after climbing the stairs and reaching the landing, where his cloak would curl around the newel post as he hastened across the passage and into the spare bedroom before disappearing into the wall which was shared with the house next door. Occasionally he had been glimpsed in the house next door but his preferred haunt was the Old Pest House. Although he passed through walls with ease, *'George'* preferred the spare bedroom door to be left open. If it was shut at night, it would be found wide open the next morning. Nervous guests who found their door opening in the night were told by the family that the lock was faulty to avoid alarming them, even though it worked perfectly well.

On a shelf on the stairs there was a row of Victorian cranberry glasses. Almost every morning they were found rearranged in pairs even though none of the family had touched them. They were frequently found like this by Mrs Mills the lady of the house who was the earliest riser and had been the last to bed the night before. Mrs Mills habitually put them back where she preferred them, only to find them moved again the next day.

'George' appeared to have a definite route through the house which began in the downstairs passage and past a row of hat pegs where the family, all of

whom were keen riders, kept their hard hats. In the morning the hats would be found flung to the floor in the hall. Picking them up and replacing them, became another regular morning chore for Mrs Mills. When the family redecorated, they found another place for the pegs away from 'George's' route and after this the hats were never disturbed again.

When the family made the decision to sell up and move out to the country there were clear signs of 'George's' disapproval and during the latter part of their occupation, his activity tried their patience. Pictures which had stood firmly for years fell down from the walls, the barn wall collapsed inexplicably and as the family resolutely continued packing, the dining room ceiling fell in on them. The family have not experienced any further paranormal activity in their new home a few miles outside Windsor and confess that they miss old 'George' and his mischievous ways. The Old Pest House has now been converted into offices and is no longer a private dwelling. It is not known how the ghost gets on with its new companions.

Nearby in Victoria Street, the **Windsor Liberal Club** is housed in the former Windsor Infirmary which served the town between 1857 until 1909 when the King Edward VII Hospital was built. After the First World War part of the Infirmary was used as a home for old soldiers and sailors but this along with most of the original building was demolished in 1973. The only part which remained was a two-storey section of the building which included a former Victorian four-bed accident ward known as the Barry Ward. This was later converted into the Liberal Club. There were several reports of strange events reported by the members and management. Roy Kirtland and his sister Beryl Hunt who ran the club for many years heard inexplicable banging coming from the old Barry Ward and the gas tap which controlled the beer flow was always being turned off. This has been checked several times by the brewery who could find no fault in it or any rational explanation for it. Customers joked that it was the ghost of a member of the Temperance Society who disapproved of the former hospital being used to serve alcohol. An armchair at the far end of the bar nearest to the Barry Ward was frequently moved and banging was heard coming through the walls even though there was no apparent cause for it. One Sunday afternoon Roy and two other customers heard the banging persist for around six hours with no regular pattern to it. There were no doors or windows open that could have accounted for it. No-one ventured down to the ward to investigate whilst the activity was going on as they were deterred by an 'unwelcoming atmosphere' and they were afraid of what they might have found. Several of the barmen left because of the strange noises and sudden cold spots which were felt in the bar. Dogs have cowered when the banging starts and refuse to go anywhere near the old ward.

Roy and Beryl also heard the rasping sound of a man's voice rambling incoherently. One customer from Slough spent the night in the bar due to severe weather which prevented him from travelling home. The next morning Beryl found him in a state of shock having clearly experienced something during the night which had caused him to flee the bar and shelter elsewhere in the building. He steadfastly refused to talk about what had taken place and told her never to mention the subject again.

Although the cause of the haunting is not known, the Windsor Infirmary did have its share of misfortune, or at least the doctors who worked there did. Dr J. W. St. John Lucas succumbed to scarlet fever in January 1871. Dr Samuel Turrell died suddenly of a cerebral haemorrhage whilst working in the Infirmary in October 1882 and in October 1894 Surgeon Philip Williams died of septicaemia after pricking his finger during an operation.

The infirmary was also the scene of untold carnage and suffering on 16 June 1900 when the West of England express crashed into a stationary train at Slough railway station. 120 passengers were badly injured, 11 of whom were taken for emergency treatment to the Windsor Infirmary and one of them died in the Barry Ward. Perhaps it is the restless spirits of these poor souls which still haunt this site.

The upper floor of the **New British School** building in Victoria Road was the scene of several reported hauntings. Before its demolition in the 1980s the school was used as the Borough Education office. Members of staff reported hearing footsteps in an empty room above, perhaps the ghost of Joseph Chariott the Victorian philanthropist who built the place in 1841 or perhaps even a long-forgotten master who lived above the school. No further activity had been reported at the modern offices which now stand on the site.

At **Long Walk House** in King's Road the ghost of an old woman was seen for many years. The house had a reputation for being unlucky after misfortune befell many of its occupants. A succession of families found it impossible to thrive at the house and fled blaming the bad aura of the house, and eventually it became used as a YWCA hostel. In the 1970s one of the wardens reported seeing the ghost of an old woman in a grey bonnet and black dress walking at the back of the house, which appeared to dissolve into thin air. Long Walk House was later demolished and a new hostel was built nearby which appears to have laid the ghost to rest.

The **Princess Margaret Hospital** in Osborne Road was originally intended to be a luxury hotel but the development in the 1970s was dogged by a series of hauntings. The ghostly events began after the initial excavations were made and it was rumoured that an ancient mass grave had been disturbed when laying the foundations. Before long there were a number of accidents on the site and several workers fled after claiming to have seen ghoulish figures. Electrical equipment began to malfunction and a series of setbacks gave the development the reputation of being cursed. The problems were compounded when contractors began to walk off the job in numbers, citing an evil atmosphere as their reason for refusal to work. Dogged by bad luck the hotel was never finished before the consortium went bankrupt. It was subsequently taken over by another developer and the layout reconfigured and converted into the Princess Margaret Hospital. Since then no further problems with unwelcome spirits have been made public.

The ghost of a 'Grey Lady' has been said to haunt the **Royal Adelaide Hotel**, an elegant Georgian building overlooking the Long Walk at 46 Kings Road. Those who have seen the spectre attest to it bearing a strong resemblance to Queen Adelaide for whom the house was originally built in the 1830s. Adelaide was a minor German princess who married the boorish Duke of Clarence, twenty-seven years her senior after only meeting him for the first time the week before the wedding in 1818. Through an unexpected twist of fate, the heavy drinking and foul-mouthed Duke became King William IV on the death of his brother George IV in 1830.

His long-suffering wife became Queen and was devoted to William, even giving a warm welcome and a good home to his ten illegitimate children and their Irish actress mother Dorothea Jordan, with whom he had a twenty-year affair. One of the descendants of their union is Old Etonian Conservative Prime Minister David Cameron.

Queen Adelaide died in 1849 and was buried at St George's Chapel, forever immortalised in the South Australian city which bears her name.

Royal Adelaide Hotel, Kings Road. The home of Queen Adelaide in death as well as life?
Courtesy of Mr John E. Hancock

Chapter 12
SHADES AROUND ST LEONARD'S ROAD

LATE ONE NIGHT two local men were driving home down **St Leonard's Road** towards the direction of King Edward VII Hospital. From out of nowhere a woman suddenly appeared in the middle of the road directly in front of their car. Although the driver slammed on the brakes they were too close to avoid hitting her and both heard a bang as the car struck a solid object. They both leapt out of the car expecting to find a body lying on the road and were mystified to discover there was no-one there and no damage to the car.

The old operating theatre at **King Edward VII Hospital** is said to be haunted by Sir Joseph Skeffington, the well-known surgeon who lived nearby and whose shadowy figure has been seen standing in the corner, as if still overseeing medical procedures. Another medical ghost is to be found at the former nurses' quarters at nearby Frances Road. Nurses living here in the 1970s reported seeing figures moving around the house at night and hearing bangs come from empty rooms.

In the 1920s, a house in **Vansittart Road** was occupied by Mr Webb a local butcher and his wife. They had a resident ghost who made a habit of knocking on the front door. This was witnessed by several people who visited them and was invariably followed by the sound of ghostly footsteps mounting their staircase. It was believed to be the shade of a former resident who continued with his homecoming ritual even after death. Although this troubled their visitors, Mr and Mrs Webb took it very much in their stride and learned to live with it. It is not known whether these phenomena continue to this day.

The punctual ghost of a house in nearby **Trinity Place** is also a creature of habit. The resident recalled how her father, cigar in hand would always open the kitchen door at 6.15pm and ask *'Is dinner ready yet?'* After his death, on several occasions when she was in the kitchen she would smell cigar smoke and when she glanced at the clock it was always at 6.15pm. This was also experienced by a visitor who thought her friend was smoking cigars. Again this was at 6.15pm.

A few doors away some years ago, a woman living in Trinity Place was disturbed by the presence of a ghostly heavy hand felt on her shoulder whilst she lay sleeping. She leapt out of bed, terrified but found the room empty. She was told by a neighbour that her house had been the scene of a gruesome murder during the Second World War when a woman was strangled there, although the identity of the victim remains unknown.

Ghosts are often associated with dark places and the night time but occasionally they are seen in broad daylight. Such was the case in the 1960s when the owner of a Georgian house in **Gloucester Place**, Mrs Phoebe Mumford was working in the garden on a beautiful sunny day when she looked up and saw a man in a cap dressed in 1920s' style clothing approaching her. As he reached a point about three or four feet away from her, he disappeared. Mr and Mrs Mumford had no idea who their garden ghost was and he was never seen in the house, although they often experienced the sound of a tinkling bell in the house. Gloucester Place is a handsome and peaceful part of Windsor and yet surprisingly many residents have reported a feeling of evil, not in their homes but in the road outside, particularly at the far end. The cause for this feeling is not known but several people have found it so overpowering that they have sold up and moved away.

On 20 November 1880 another ghost was reported to have been seen in broad daylight by a group of children on their way to school. In a locked and unoccupied premises, previously a butcher's shop, on the corner of **William Street**, a ghostly presence was seen which attracted the attention of a large crowd. Many people witnessed the shadowy spectre as it moved around the building and such a large crowd gathered that police had to be called to prevent disorder. A forced entry was made and the premises searched but nothing was found.

The crowd proved difficult to disperse and was reminiscent of the phenomenon known as 'flash mobs', which developed throughout the eighteenth and nineteenth centuries where unruly crowds quickly developed at the scene of an incident. They appeared to be particularly quick to develop at the scene of any supernatural occurrences, the most famous of which was the 'Cock Lane Ghost' in London in 1768. This haunting was witnessed by hundreds including notable figures like Robert Walpole the first British Prime Minister and Dr Johnson. Although it was later denounced as a hoax, some modern commentators suggest the original poltergeist activity was genuine but was subsequently exploited by the owner of the house to cash-in on the vast crowds which it generated.

In the case of the William Street ghost, no explanation was ever found and although spectators returned to the scene for several days, no further sighting was ever made and the curious incident remains a mystery.

Chapter 13
CREEPY CLEWER

ALTHOUGH CLEWER HAS been subsumed in Windsor's sprawling development in recent years, for centuries it had an identity of its own as a riverside village. The original name *Clifwara* means cliff dwellers and refers to the original medieval settlers who lived below the hill on which the Castle was situated, and then known as Clewer Hill. Although the phantoms of Windsor Castle may be more well-known, this part of town also has a wide variety of fascinating ghost stories which have been neglected for many years.

The **Swan Public House** at Clewer stands on the site of a medieval coaching inn which served travellers as they journeyed down Mill Lane which formed the main road between Maidenhead and Windsor. This became the principal crossing point across the Thames. The current building dates from the eighteenth century and provided ale, food and simple accommodation, together with a coaching service and fresh horses. The stables still stand at the back of the pub, while a tunnel from the pub yard to the historic church of St Andrew's is still believed to be intact.

Until the nineteenth century, the inn was used as the local coroner's court, with a brisk trade in bodies from the river. The mortuary was at the rear of the inn, and the landlord was also a part-time mortician. The pub is reputed to be haunted by the ghost of one of the assistant morticians who was a regular customer and has been seen in the bar revisiting his former 'local'.

Clewer Lodge was home to the ghost of a crying child, and even after its demolition, the plaintive moans of the ghostly child could be heard in the place where it stood. In the 1970s, police houses were built on the site and several residents of Peel Close reported hearing the sound of a crying girl, although its location could never be pinpointed. One of the houses in particular was frequently left empty for long periods as the tenants found it had a cold and unwelcoming atmosphere and strange unaccountable noises were heard.

Clewer Hill House also now demolished, had a spare-bedroom which was never used because of its oppressive atmosphere. The maid used to hurry through her work in the room in order to spend as little time as possible there. It has been suggested that some unknown tragedy occurred there but details are sadly lacking.

The Nurses Training College at Clewer had a friendly resident ghost who was called *'Emily'*. She was been responsible for opening and closing doors and windows in contravention of official instructions and one night her footsteps were heard walking along the landing and knocking on the door of a student who was suffering from a bad cough. This was overheard by a nurse in the room next door who assumed it was someone arriving with a cough remedy as the coughing ceased after the visit. The next morning it was revealed the coughing colleague had no knowledge of the night-time visitor. On another occasion a student nurse reported an invisible figure trying to get into bed with her although perhaps it was *'Emily'* trying to tuck her in.

The **Church of England Children's Society Home** once stood at Clewer and was run by an order of Anglican nuns known as the Sisterhood of St John the Baptist. One of the bedrooms there had to be turned into an office because of the bad atmosphere. Strange mists appeared without explanation and the temperature would drop dramatically. It is alleged that one of the nuns once hanged herself in the parkland nearby and thereafter one of the rooms was characterised by a malevolent and oppressive atmosphere which was so palpable that no-one would sleep there. Up until its closure and subsequent demolition, the nuns found it difficult to recruit cleaners to work at the home and when they did, they insisted on working in pairs.

In 1977 reports circulated of a ghost at The **Black Horse Pub** on the Dedworth Road believed to be the ghost of a former customer. Although nothing was ever seen, there were several poltergeist activities including glasses moving of their own accord. Barmaids were also frequently accosted by the over-familiar ghost who pinched their bottoms as they served behind the bar.

On the military estate of **Broom Farm** in 2000, the parents of a pre-school child were alarmed when they overheard him talking to an invisible visitor at the family home. As they watched with hackles rising they heard the little boy telling the entity to *'Keep away from my mommy and daddy.'* When asked who he was talking to, the child replied *'An old man who wants to get you.'* It is understood that the family was re-housed by the military a short time later.

During the 1990s in **Vale Road** Dedworth, Mrs Ethel Griffiths reported seeing the ghost of an old man appear from the wall behind her bed and walk across the bedroom. Ethel stated:

'I saw him on several occasions always when I was in bed. He would appear from the wall behind my head and walk alongside the bed. He was dressed in 1920s clothing with a waistcoat and would be looking at his watch as though he was waiting for something. He seemed unaware that I was even there.'

The identity of the ghostly old man with a pocket watch remains unknown.

Number **6 Windmill Close**, Dedworth is an unassuming bungalow built in the 1950s and for many years up until 2004 was the home of Mrs Trudy

Dunsmore. In the latter years of her life Trudy sadly suffered from early stage Alzheimer's disease and began to exhibit strange behaviour which friends and family put down to her condition.

She began to sew up the bedroom curtains every night because of the people in the garden watching her. She started to sit in the hallway and when asked why, answered, *'The people don't like me sitting in the lounge.'*

Alex Crewe, her daughter recalled:

'She complained for five years about the house but I'm sad to say we took very little notice, believing her to be confused. Eventually she went into a nursing home and a short time later I moved into her house with my children when my marriage ended.'

Within a short time Alex began to experience strange activity at the house and saw ghostly figures around the house which defied explanation.

'At first I noticed that a person regularly walked down the side of the house past a frosted glass window in the living room. The figure was clear to see and in the evenings set off the sensor light on the garage, but it never arrived at the back door or returned past the window. When I went out to check there was never anyone there. This happened several times every day.'

'Late one night I heard people whispering outside the bedroom window and the sound of footsteps moving about. I looked outside but there was nothing there. When I went back into the house the whispering started again. This continued late at night for months as though invisible figures were having a conversation right beside the window.'

Alex also heard big-band swing music playing inside the bathroom late almost every night.

Alex said *'It wasn't the neighbours; it definitely originated inside the house but could only be heard in the bathroom. It couldn't be heard outside the bathroom at all or in the attic above it – just inside the bathroom. It was bizarre.'*

Alex lived in the bungalow for almost two years and these events happened continuously throughout her time there. She was never frightened by the strange phenomena but was occasionally unsettled by them and often wondered whether the ghostly occurrences were behind some of her mother's strange behaviour. She moved out and the house was rented-out twice over the subsequent four years.

'Both times I never mentioned the odd events to the tenants but both sets reported the same things happening to them. The first couple quite liked living in a "haunted house" the second lot did not and only stayed a year.'

The house was finally sold to new owners but it is not known whether the strange supernatural activity continues to this day.

Chapter 14

THE WINDSOR 'WEREWOLF'

IN NOVEMBER 2000 two Windsor police officers had a nocturnal encounter with a strange wolf-like creature seen at the edge at the Thames near to the Windsor Canoe Club. PCs Tom Walters and Lucy Palmer were on a routine patrol during the early hours of the morning and could not believe their eyes when they caught the looming figure of an enormous wolf-like beast in their headlights in the Windsor Leisure Pool car park in Stovell Road. Startled by their sudden arrival, the beast turned and loped away towards the river disappearing into the shadows leaving the bewildered officers wondering what they had just seen.

Lucy said *'It looked too big to be a dog and seemed irritated that we had disturbed it. It had an odd gait and walked towards the river where it vanished. Tom and I were dumb-struck and just looked at each other as if to say what the hell was that? There was no way either of us was getting out to check. It looked for all the world like a big wolf so we made a note of it just in case but no-one else ever reported anything.'*

In fact, unbeknown to the officers, an identical beast had been spotted by one of their colleagues a decade previously, 6 miles further along the Thames at Boulter's Lock in Maidenhead.

One cold and damp night in February 1990, PC Gail Emptage was coming to the end of her late night anti-burglary cycle patrol and decided to do a final tour along the river. She cycled along Ray Mead Road from Maidenhead Bridge towards Cookham. It was half past midnight and as silent as the grave with not a soul in sight as the mist blew across her path from the river. As she passed Boulter's Lock she was startled by a sudden movement coming from the direction of the Thames towpath.

Gail recalled: *'I had just cycled past Boulter's Lock when I heard something move on the riverbank. I saw what I thought was large shaggy dog. It was so big that my first thought was that it must be a St Bernard. As it loped across the road just 20 feet ahead of me, it was clearly illuminated by the street lighting and I could see it had the appearance of a huge wolf. It had a thick shaggy coat which was dark grey in colour. The texture of its coat was matted not unlike the fleece of a "Herdwick" Sheep. There was no doubt in my mind that it was solid and real.'*

The creature walked across her path into the mouth of the junction with Lock Avenue opposite, and then suddenly stopped. Its ears pricked up almost as if it had just sensed her presence. Gail stopped her bike in the middle of the road and froze as the beast slowly turned its head in her direction and stared at her over its shoulder.

Gail recalled: *'My blood ran cold. It had an air of arrogance and almost human intelligence. It had canine features with a long muzzle and upright pointed ears but what terrified me most were its eyes. They glowed with an intense yellow-green luminosity and fixed their glare on me for several seconds. They were like two torch beams – nothing like any dog I had ever seen. It was almost daring me to approach. I don't mind admitting I was terrified. I turned my bike round and pedalled as fast as my legs could carry me back to the police station. I never went down that stretch of road again alone after dark.'*

There are striking similarities in these sightings seen by professional witnesses over a decade apart which has given rise to speculation that a wolf-like cryptid roams the banks of the historic Thames.

These are not isolated reports and for centuries sightings of strange wolf-like beasts, stalking this part of Berkshire have featured in local folklore. 'The White Hound of Fiennes' was reported as late as the 1980s, running through the ancient Berkshire woodland before vanishing instantly as though it had run behind a black sheet.

Chapter 15
THE CLEWER POLTERGEIST

IN 1848 THE world was taken by storm by two sisters, Maggie and Kate Fox who from their haunted cabin in Hydesville USA, began communicating with spirits of the dead through rapping. This was the genesis of spiritualism which quickly spread across the western world and gave rise to the images of séances that we now associate with Victorian mediumship.

Six years before the Fox sisters' revelation, Clewer was the home to an equally amazing display of poltergeist activity which rivalled anything that had taken place at Hydesville. The story is now long-forgotten and yet at the time attracted widespread attention. The paranormal activity continued for many months and was witnessed by dozens of eminent people, whipping up the local townsfolk into a state of considerable excitement.

The Clewer poltergeist case began in January 1842 when Mr and Mrs Wright, a middle-aged couple recently retired from business, moved into Want's Cottage set in its own grounds in Clewer just a mile from Windsor Castle. It was an idyllic setting but within a short time their new rented home gave them cause for concern. They began to hear strange tapping sounds and before long, reports began to emerge that their house was haunted by a spirit who was plaguing them with unearthly noises at all hours of the night and day. The ghostly sounds were described as like a person rapping their knuckles at a door panel for two or three seconds.

The desperate couple invited in a group of doubting locals to hear the phenomenon for themselves. Their scepticism quickly evaporated when they witnessed the tapping noises, loud enough to be heard 500 yards away, emanating from a door which led from the kitchen into the water-closet.

As word of the extraordinary events spread, the cottage was visited by a string of psychics and scientists, all of whom came with pet theories but left mystified by what they saw and heard. The loud rapping noise was heard several times a day by independent witnesses and occasionally, it was reported that the candles in the house burnt with a blue flame when the noise sounded.

Such was the notoriety of Want's Cottage that local police, magistrates and clergy spend considerable time there in an attempt to unravel the mystery, but left bewildered.

A concerted effort was made to fully investigate the phenomenon and track down the cause once and for all. During one weekend a delegation of eminent and learned local figures and other independent observers descended on the house to conduct a vigil. These included the Rev. Gould, Vicar of St Stephen's church and Major-General Clement Hill, a distinguished military figure who had served with Wellington at Waterloo and who lived nearby.

The assembled throng did not have to wait long before the rapping started on the toilet door. Although they were standing within three yards of the door and in plain sight, they all confirmed that not a soul was near it and the rest of the family were elsewhere in the house.

In the months that followed the supernatural noises continued and Want's Cottage was visited by a succession of 'men of science' intent on solving the mystery. The prime suspect was considered to be the 'foul air' in the plumbing and at great inconvenience to the Wrights, the water closet was removed, the flooring taken up and the ground excavated to a depth of 5 feet but still the noises continued, increasing in regularity and more violent than ever. Mr Manly the parish sexton attended and with a grave-diggers sounding iron, sounded the ground both inside and outside the premises without revealing any clue as to the cause of the knocking, which continued on throughout. Scientific analysis was even made of the water from the drains and surrounding ditches but nothing out of the ordinary was discovered.

A series of rudimentary experiments was conducted as people tested out their theories as to the cause of this bizarre occurrence. A small chip of wood was placed on the panel of the door and was seen to fall when the noise began, suggesting an invisible hand banging the door. Mr Wright's son arrived from Newbury and in the presence of independent witnesses fastened up the door by means of a piece of wire. After the noise had ceased the wire was found to have been snapped and the door forced inwards. At one point the force of the banging was so violent that the door was broken off its hinges and pushed to the back of the closet, and yet the knocking continued precisely the same as it had before.

By now, in the absence of a rational explanation, people became convinced the only explanation was a supernatural one. Mrs Roberts, a neighbour who lived two streets away, had been so disturbed by the noises that she gave notice to quit. Mr and Mrs Wright also began to wonder how much longer they could live with this turbulent spirit. Rumours began to circulate that the previous occupant had been seen vacating the premises in *a very mysterious manner'* and speculation grew that the knocking was the restless ghost of someone who had been murdered at the cottage.

Although this was never given any credence by the authorities, in the course of their investigations, the house was searched many times and no evidence of foul play was ever discovered.

The landlady of the house, Mrs Stokes, having read about the events in the newspaper arrived from London to see for herself what was going on. She witnessed on three or four occasions the ghostly knocking whilst in the presence of at least five other people who were totally unconnected with the house or the family.

Paranormal sightseers and scientific minds alike came and went over a period of six months during which time the family became worn down by the attention and the incessant knocking.

By June of that year Want's Cottage had gained such notoriety that a permanent police presence was posted at the premises. One poor constable stationed there noted that he had heard distinct knockings on thirteen occasions during his twelve hour shift whilst he was standing just 6 feet from the door and with no-one else in the vicinity. The family finally announced that they could bear it no more and began to pack up their belongings for departure the next day. The following morning the tapping recommenced loudly at 7.30am as if in a gesture of mocking triumph. With the policeman still in attendance the Wright family moved out of the house lock, stock and barrel, the awful noise still ringing in their ears.

Local figures, some of whom had their suspicions that this had been an elaborate hoax, were quick to take the opportunity to gain access to the property and spend a final night in the haunted house. Accompanied by a police guard they conducted a candlelight sitting around the clock from 9pm until 8am the next morning. Nothing whatsoever was heard and neither did their candles or log fire burn blue. They concluded that this was proof positive that clever trickery had been afoot all along.

There is one other explanation however, which has not previously been explored and involves the other hitherto unmentioned members of the Wright's family. Research has uncovered that Mr and Mrs Wright had two teenage daughters who lived with them in the house. This has obvious parallels to the Fox sisters at Hydesville. Whilst it is possible that the daughters were responsible for faking the phenomenon, it seems unlikely given the detailed descriptions of the activity and the independent witnesses to it.

More likely is a phenomenon which parapsychologists call *subconscious telekinesis*. This theory asserts that poltergeist activity is in fact caused unwittingly by a human agent. Researchers believe that a troubled adolescent unconsciously manipulates objects using psychokinetic energy in the brain. The presence of teenage girls is a characteristic frequently found in poltergeist 'hauntings' most notably in the Enfield Poltergeist case in 1977.

The case concluded with the Wright family being lambasted in the press for having contrived the phenomenon themselves, although no motive for this was ever proffered, much less any evidence of their guilt. The case was dubbed a second '*Cock Lane Ghost*' in reference to the famous haunting in London which Dr Johnson had denounced as a fraud some eighty years previously. The record does not show whether the ghostly knocking noises accompanied the Wright family to their new abode but if it did, it would hardly be surprising if they chose to remain silent about it.

Want's Cottage never managed to shake off it's supernatural reputation and although no further poltergeist activity was ever subsequently reported there, Mrs Stokes was unable to find another tenant willing to live in the 'haunted house' and it remained empty until it was sold and later demolished.

Who knows, had the daughters attempted to communicate with the spirits in the way that the Fox sisters did six years later, Clewer could well have become the birthplace of spiritualism.

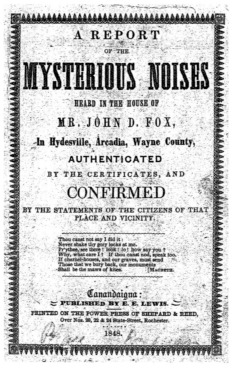

A contemporary pamphlet reporting the Hydesville poltergeist. Wikimedia Commons

Chapter 16
THE 'SPRING-HEELED JACK' OF SPITAL GRAVEYARD

ANOTHER LONG-FORGOTTEN ghost story associated with Clewer became known as The 'Spring Heeled Jack' of Spital Graveyard after the notorious phantom which first appeared in London in 1837. During the cold dark winter of February 1859 the townsfolk of Windsor were alarmed by a series of sightings of a monstrous spectre near the gates of the newly consecrated cemetery at St Leonards Road in an isolated area of the town known as Spital. Over a period of several weeks, the lonely road leading out of town past the Combermere cavalry barracks and out into Windsor Great Park was the subject of frightful nightly apparitions which struck terror into those who saw it.

One of the first people to witness this was the sexton, the resident gravedigger who lived and worked at the cemetery. One night whilst digging a grave, he felt an overwhelmingly malign presence watching him. As the hackles on his neck began to rise, he turned around to see a horrifying figure sitting on the gate at the entrance to the burial ground fixing him with a malevolent stare. He described it as 8 or 9 feet tall and shrouded in white. The affrighted sexton fled screaming from the graveyard in a state of panic.

Many believed he had disturbed the ancient resting place of an evil spirit whilst digging graves in the cemetery, whilst others blamed it on a drop too much of his nightly tipple.

However in the three weeks that followed the enormous foreboding figure was seen by several different people. After each horrifying appearance the ghost would disappear without trace into the cemetery. Lone women in particular appeared to be most victimised but several men were also terrorised by the figure.

The numbers of sightings became so numerous that the cemetery rapidly became a 'no-go' area, particularly after dark. The local borough police came under considerable pressure to act. Their initial reticence to do so quickly subsided when matters escalated and victims were physically molested and injured. A young groom returning late to his master's home one night was attacked by the towering ghoul and set about unmercifully, before being left battered and bruised in a ditch as the ghost disappeared once again into the night fog.

The situation was getting out of control and the growing clamour for action became deafening. In response to the public outcry, and to counter threats of vigilante action by the terrified community, the borough police chief finally took action and deployed a lone policeman, PC John Smith-Noble to lay the ghost of Spital cemetery to rest.

Armed only with a whistle and a truncheon the anxious young PC Noble lay in wait quaking with fear and trepidation. Never before had he been instructed to arrest a phantom felon. For two hours there was nothing save the hooting of owls and the occasional flutter of bats. But then just as midnight chimed – there rising in front of him from behind a bush was the looming ghostly white figure which he had dreaded encountering. The diaphanous spectre rose further into the air before the adrenaline-fuelled officer, screaming in fright, launched himself at the figure and brought it to the ground.

A graveyard ghost from an early C19th engraving. Wikimedia Commons

After several minutes of violent struggle with the unearthly, but very solid shade, the police officer suppressed the monster with a combination of brute force and truncheon blows. As the mist cleared his supernatural quarry was revealed to him. Lying dazed on the ground was the unmistakable body of a man dressed in women's clothing armed with a loaded pistol! The bewildered officer dragged the man to his feet and demanded an explanation from the hapless moaning figure.

The man was no less than Private William Rush of the 2nd Life Guards, the elite mounted regiment of the Household Cavalry responsible for the protection of Queen Victoria. Mary Rush, his wife, had been one of the women attacked by the phantom whilst on her way home some days previously. Trooper Rush, frustrated at the lack of police action had decided to take matters into his own hands and had donned one of his wife's frocks in order to lure the graveyard beast into the open. At least this was the story the magistrates heard. As far as the police were concerned, they had got their man and he was hauled up before the police court on charges of breach of the peace, assault and possession of firearms.

At the court there was pandemonium as people flocked to see the incarcerated phantom. Threats were shouted from the public gallery to horsewhip him if he was ever found in the vicinity again. Trooper Rush adamantly maintained his innocence that he was not 'Spring-Heeled Jack' but was in fact performing a public service in trying to shoot it. This was corroborated by his wife who lent the strapping 6-footer one of her dresses for the purpose. The Windsor authorities were however unconvinced, and Trooper Rush was found guilty on all counts and handed over to the military at Combermere Barracks for a court martial to take place. He was sentenced to a substantial period of imprisonment in a military jail. PC Noble became a local hero for tackling the armed spectre and this feather in his cap undoubtedly contributed towards his later promotion to Sergeant.

Back in Windsor opinion was somewhat divided. Although most applauded the police for their success in capturing the graveyard spook, others believed the soldier was innocent and that the creature was still haunting the Spital graveyard. For several nights after Trooper Rush's arrest, townsfolk armed with makeshift weapons lay in wait but nothing ever came. Some concluded that this proved his guilt, others that the prayers and blessings said in the cemetery by the local vicar had successfully laid the ghost to rest. Whether Trooper Rush was the victim of a miscarriage of justice or a disturbed sociopath will probably never be known, but suffice to say that the 'Spring-Heeled Jack' of Spital graveyard has lain dormant now for over a century and a half.

Chapter 17
TANGO TANGO NINE ZERO – WHERE ARE YOU?

A SUPERNATURAL ENCOUNTER during a night shift in 2008 along a lonely road on the outskirts of Windsor left two officers from the Thames Valley Roads Policing Department with an experience they will never forget.

As Tango Tango Nine Zero swung into Tarbay Lane, Oakley Green, PC Stanhope and Sergeant Keyes glanced at the dashboard clock. It was 2.30am; it had been a quiet night – a very quiet night. Their efforts to find stolen cars had so far proved fruitless. PC Stanhope flicked onto main beam and drove slowly along the unmade gravel path, the car rocking from side to side as it lurched in and out of potholes. Then the headlights caught something. It was a silver hatchback parked up on the side of the road. The engine was off and there were no lights on.

As they drew closer, they could just make out the silhouette of two figures inside. Believing it to be worthy of a check they pulled over and approached the vehicle. As the window was wound down, they were surprised to see the occupants were a middle-aged couple wrapped in scarves and woolly hats with a flask of tea and a pack of sandwiches on their lap.

When asked for an explanation, the couple told them they were ghost-hunting as the lane was a psychic hotspot and well-known for paranormal activity. The officers exchanged knowing glances and bade them farewell. They returned to their patrol car sniggering and smirking.

Continuing up Tarbay Lane, they passed a thickly wooded area about half way up and the radio traffic suddenly stopped as if it had been unplugged. Their hi-tech dashboard, normally illuminated with an array of video and computer screens, also went black. PC Stanhope stopped the car and they looked at each other as the smiles drained away from their faces.

Sgt Keyes pushed buttons and flicked switches, but nothing responded. Everything was completely dead. The officers were bewildered. This had never happened before. The pride of the Roads Policing fleet was completely without any means of communication. There was total silence in the vehicle. The officers looked around them at the dense woodland and suddenly became very frightened and PC Stanhope felt the hackles rise on the back of his neck and felt the need to get away.

He accelerated away up the hill and as they left the wooded area the welcome sound of radio traffic returned and the computer systems burst back into electronic life. With hearts pounding they reached the end of the lane and stopped the car at the dead end. With great relief the two officers got out of the car to get their breath and have a cigarette to calm their nerves.

After a couple of minutes the officers got back into their car, turned it around and went back down the hill towards the main road. They were starting to relax when as soon as they reached the exact same wooded spot, their radio and recording systems again shut down completely for the second time. They looked at each other with widened eyes. Before they had a chance to say a word – Bang! From the direction of the woods, something heavy struck the driver's window with such force that they thought the window was coming in.

PC Stanhope 'floored' the accelerator, spinning the wheels on the gravel as they careered down the hill. As they left the wooded area the radio, computer and video systems once more crackled back into life as they sped past the bemused couple sipping tea in their car. He screeched out onto the main road and accelerated through Oakley Green village.

After an adrenaline-fuelled couple of minutes with hearts still racing they pulled over into a lay-by. They both sat in silence, breathing deeply and trying to process what they had experienced. After a moment Sergeant Keyes broke the silence. *'Stan – we're going back to the nick for a cuppa … and this never happened OK?'* PC Stanhope nodded in agreement as he picked up the radio. *'Tango Tango Nine Zero to control. Can you show us going for a quick comfort break? Over and out.'*

PC Stanhope never spoke about this experience until six years later and still shudders when he thinks about it. To this day he has never been back along Tarbay Lane and confided that he was so spooked by the incident, that if a job ever came in from there, he would avoid it like the plague.

What neither of the officers knew at the time, but perhaps the ghost-watching couple did, was that there had been previously reported supernatural activity in Tarbay Lane at Nightingale Cottage, near to where the officers had their bizarre encounter. The cottage dates back to Elizabethan times and was for many years the home of the late Dr Esther Rickards OBE, a down-to-earth and well respected GP and dog show judge whose family had lived there for three generations.

In *Windsor Ghosts and Other Berkshire Hauntings,* Angus Macnaghten relates that the cottage is home to the ghost of an Elizabethan nurse, sensed rather than seen, on several occasions but only when children were in residence at the sixteenth-century farmhouse. Dr Rickards and the family were firmly convinced that the kindly soul looked after the welfare of any children in the house. In cold weather when the children went upstairs to close the windows they found that the ghost had been there before them and they were already shut.

Tarbay Lane it seems is home to more than one paranormal presence, some more benign than others.

Chapter 18
WITCHCRAFT AND WICKEDNESS

IN ELIZABETHAN ENGLAND a belief in witchcraft and superstition was widespread and there was paranoia around plots to assassinate the Queen either by physical or supernatural means. In 1578 three female wax figures were found buried in a dung heap in London. The figures were stuck with broom bristles where the heart would exist on human body. Elizabeth was known to have a particular dread of witchcraft involving graven images and fearing another treasonous plot involving sorcery, a nationwide witch-hunt began.

This was the context when a coven of witches was uncovered operating in Windsor, in the Queen's own back garden. A stableman at a local inn was in the habit of giving a few coins to local ladies at the almshouses. One day one of the women Elizabeth Stile made her displeasure felt at the pitiful donation he made to her and instead of expressing her gratitude, cursed him. Soon afterwards he fell ill with pains in his limbs and this was attributed to witchcraft. He was told that he could be cured if he could draw the blood of the witch who cast the spell. He promptly sought her out and attacked her, scratching her until the blood flowed and he recovered.

Soon gossip began to circulate that Elizabeth Stile and several other women at the almshouse were part of a coven which used to meet at Windsor *'in the pits at the back of Master Dodge's House.'* The Windsor coven was blamed for a number of sudden deaths including Richard Gallis the former Mayor of Windsor and landlord of The Garter Inn.

This culminated in the arrest of sixty-five-year-old Elizabeth Stile alias Rockingham, who was forced to walk the 12 miles to Reading where she was imprisoned and interrogated. Further arrests followed; Mother Dutten of Clewer, Mother Devell and Mother Margaret were rounded up on charges of sorcery and witchcraft. Under robust interrogation they confessed their

Mother Dutton of Clewer feeding her 'familiars' from a woodcut 1579.
Wikimedia Commons

deeds and implicated one Father Rosimond from Farnham Common and his daughter. Father Rosimond was never brought to trial but was believed to be the leader of the coven and was alleged to be a shape-shifter and was *'sometymes in the shape of an ape, and otherwhiles like a horse.'*

All the women were examined and found to have 'Devil's marks', further proof of their guilt. Actually these were likely to be no more than moles or birthmarks but were presented by the prosecution as extra nipples which they used to feed their evil 'familiars'.

During the trial, details of these 'familiars' were revealed to gasps of horror from the public gallery. These evil spirits also participated in the black arts and ownership was proof of witchcraft. Mother Dutton's familiar was a toad which she kept in her herb garden and fed with blood from her flank, Mother Devell's familiar appeared as a black cat called *'Gille'* which she fed with milk mingled with her own blood. Mother Margaret fed her familiar *'Ginnie'* with breadcrumbs mixed with blood whilst Elizabeth Stile kept a diabolical rat with the unlikely name of *'Philip'*, which she fed with blood from her right wrist and which was described in court as *'in very deede a wicked spirite'*.

According to Elizabeth Stile's confession, which if not made under torture was certainly made under the threat of violence, she claimed she was led into witchcraft by Mothers Dutten and Devell. The three would meet at 11 o'clock at night to pledge themselves to service to the Devil and cast malevolent spells against anyone who angered them.

She admitted the witches had brought about the death of a farmer called Lanckforde, one of Lanckforde's maids, a butcher called Switcher and another butcher called Masclyn. They had also murdered Richard Gallis, the former Mayor of Windsor. The deaths were brought about by making effigies of the victims in red wax *'about a span long and three or four fingers broad'* and then piercing them with hawthorn. The witches were also said to have placed a spell on Humfrey Hosie and his wife, Richard Milles and John Mathynglise who all became ill as a result.

Further evidence was brought against them about spells they had cast at the request of people in the town. George Whittyng, servant of Matthew Glover of Eton testified that he asked them to harm a man called Foster and she saw them make a wax effigy and Mother Devell sent her familiar *'Gille'* to *'plague him and spare him not.'* Foster was promptly taken ill but restored by Mother Dutton, when close to death, although one of his cows died.

No treason was ever discovered, but in front of a baying crowd all four witches were found guilty of the malefic murders and other sorcery and executed by hanging at Abingdon gibbet on 26 February 1579. Thus ended the remarkable trial of the 'Windsor Witches', an infamous case of hysterical persecution of people whose only crime was to be eccentric.

A quarter of a century later another monarch became involved in a case of witchcraft which had a happier ending for the suspect. In 1603 James VI of Scotland succeeded to the English throne as James I. He had a keen interest in witchcraft and in 1597 had written a book called *Daemonologie* a re-interpretation of the earlier *Malleus Maleficarum* (The Hammer of Witches). This wide-ranging discussion of witchcraft, necromancy, possession, demons, were-wolves, fairies and ghosts became used as the standard witch-hunt manual for the prosecution of witches and led to 40 deaths for witchcraft under his reign, earning him a reputation as a fearsome oppo-nent of sorcery.

However the case of Anne Gunter in 1604 was a rare case of common-sense prevailing. Wishing to be seen as an enlightened monarch and delighting in exposing hoaxes, James took personal charge of the case of Anne Gunter, a fourteen-year-old Windsor girl who displayed symp-

Malleus Maleficarum – (The Hammer of Witches) used as the handbook for the persecution of witches.
Wikimedia Commons

toms associated with bewitchment. Hearing of the case, James ordered her to appear before him and arranged for her to be examined by Dr Edward Jorden a reputable London physician who had previously uncovered false claims. He concluded that the girl was a charlatan and when confronted by the King, she admitted her fraud claiming she was under duress from her father Brian Gunter, who had hoped to accuse a local woman of witchcraft with whom he had quarrelled. James pardoned Anne, and the wrongly-accused 'witch' happily escaped the gallows on this occasion.

Another witch saved from execution features in an intriguing witchcraft conspiracy theory concerning the founding of the Ancient and Most Noble Order of the Garter, the oldest chivalric order in the world.

New Knights of the Garter are invested at a lavish ceremony at St George's Chapel in June each year. The Order was founded, according to legend, when

Katherine, Countess of Salisbury, dropped her garter at a court ball at Windsor Castle in 1349 when dancing with King Edward III.

Tradition says that to cover the lady's embarrassment, King Edward picked up the garter, and with the words, '*Honi soit qui mal y pense*' (Shame on him who thinks this evil), buckled it onto his own leg.

However, a garter was also said to be the distinguishing badge of the chief witch of a coven and therefore the revelation proved to Edward that he was dancing with the England's most senior witch. His actions therefore were not intended to save merely her modesty, but to save her from prosecution and certain death for sorcery at the hands of his superstitious courtiers.

He later formed the Order of twenty six knights, two covens of thirteen with himself at the head. Today the monarch wears a cloak patterned with one hundred and sixty eight garters and another worn on the leg which makes thirteen times thirteen signifying the thirteen covens of England. Perhaps witchcraft did indeed influence one of our earliest Royal traditions.

Paranoia about witches was rife in Elizabethan England.
Wikimedia Commons

PART THREE
WINDSOR GREAT PARK

....

Chapter 19
HIDEOUS HERNE THE HUNTER

WINDSOR GREAT PARK forms part of the ancient hunting grounds of the Kings and Queens of England spreading out across 5000 acres of beautiful Berkshire. The historic woodland has been the location of pagan worship and mystical activity since long before the Norman Conquest. Criss-crossed by ley lines and home to some of the oldest trees in the realm, Windsor Great Park has a rich supernatural heritage.

It is also the home of one of the oldest and most famous ghosts in English folklore, Herne the Hunter. His story has been told countless times in literature most notably by Shakespeare, who chose the forest as the setting for *The Merry Wives of Windsor* which was first performed by Royal Command of Queen Elizabeth I at Windsor Castle on the evening of his birthday 23 April 1597.

In order to appreciate the numerous hauntings of this ancient forest, it is necessary to first understand the legend of Herne the Hunter who even by Shakespeare's time, was an ancient and well-recognised character.

The tale of Herne the Hunter can be traced back to the middle part of the reign of Richard II (1377 – 1399). There was a young gamekeeper named Herne whose skill in tracking and hunting was so great that it was almost supernatural. His incredible prowess quickly brought him to the attention of the King. Always accompanied by his two trademark black hounds *'of St Hubert's breed'*, Herne soon became the King's favoured hunting companion, much to the disgust of the seasoned huntsmen in the Royal entourage. One day whilst hunting in the forest a stag turned and charged Richard, killing his horse and would have killed him, had Herne not bravely intervened and jumped in between them. Although he killed the stag and saved the King, Herne was mortally gored in the process.

The King appealed to all those present, offering a huge reward for anyone who could save Herne, but the other gamekeepers, who were jealous of Herne's skill and favour with the King, were happy to see him die. Indeed

Herne the Hunter from Harrison Ainsworth's Windsor Castle *1845.*
Wikimedia Commons

Osmonde Crook, the Chief Keeper, as he drew his hunting-knife, tenderly volunteered, *'to put the suffering youth out of his misery.'* Then suddenly appeared a tall, dark man on a wild-looking black steed. This strange figure was described in most accounts as a wizard or physician named Phillip Urswick. He told the King that he could save Herne. He cut off the head of the dead hart close to the point where the neck joined the skull, and then laid it open and ordered it to be bound on the head of the wounded man.

The wizard then had him carried out on a litter made of oak wood and mistletoe to his home on Bagshot Heath where he cast a spell on Herne to cure him.

The King promised that if he recovered, he would make Herne his chief huntsman. This sat uncomfortably with the others in the King's retinue who had their own ambitions for this much-coveted title.

One night the jealous courtiers visited the wizard at Bagshot Heath and made it clear that they did not want Herne to recover. The wizard being a man of his word said that he would not renege on his promise to the King, but would arrange for his legendary hunting ability to be impaired, but this would come at a price – and that price was for them to accede to the first request Urswick made of them. Believing this to be a small price to pay, they readily agreed.

Sure enough Herne made a miraculous recovery and as promised, was honoured by the King with the title of chief huntsman and presented with a pure black horse and a silver hunting horn. But through Urswick's spell, Herne had lost all his celebrated skill as an archer and his extraordinary craft as a hunter. Reluctantly, the King found him no longer useful as a hunting companion, and quickly tired of him. Before long he fell from favour and was no longer invited to join the Royal hunt.

Herne became despondent and wondered around the forest as a wild man whilst his enemies revelled in his downfall. One night, with the stag's antlered skull fixed to his head, he hanged himself from an ancient oak tree.

A pedlar travelling from Datchet, found the grisly cadaver hanging in the forest. At that time it was believed that the spirit of a person who committed suicide was not permitted to enter heaven, and would instead remain on earth and haunt the scene of their death. By the time the King's servants, alerted by the pedlar, arrived at the tragic spot, the body was gone, and only the rope was swinging from the branch. That night, there was a terrible thunderstorm, and the very oak henceforward to be known as Herne's Oak, was blasted by lightning.

It was at this point that the curse of Herne began to truly manifest itself. The conspirators also fell from favour with the King, beginning with Osmonde Crook. His bolts and arrows flew wide of their mark, his hounds lost their scent, and his falcon would not be lured back. The same fate befell all those who succeeded him as Chief Keeper.

In desperation, they visited the wizard Urswick at Bagshot Heath and asked for his help. They were told that Herne's ghost had inhabited the great oak where he hanged himself and they would have no rest until they appeased his troubled spirit. Legend has it that he told them to gather at midnight beneath the mighty oak and await a sign.

Anxious to rid themselves of the curse, the conspirators assembled under the full moon around the ancient tree. To their amazement in a mysterious cloud of purple smoke, the wizard appeared before them and demanded that they now fulfil the promise they made to him to grant his first request. He called on them to form a band for Herne the Hunter, and to serve him as their leader. He then invoked the ghost of Herne who materialised before them

complete with terrifying horns growing from his head, astride a massive black horse with his ghostly hounds baying beside him.

Herne commanded the bewildered onlookers to follow him into the forest. Not daring to refuse, the bewitched keepers took the oath and a wild hunt commenced, which lasted until an hour before daybreak. Night after night they assembled for the same purpose at Herne's Oak and embarked upon the systematic slaughter of every deer in the forest.

The King, hearing of the nocturnal outrages and depredations, went with his guards into the forest at midnight and there, at Herne's Oak, encountered Herne himself, who demanded justice in the form of the souls of the keepers who had

The original Herne's Oak in 1793 before it was felled by George III.
© The Royal Windsor Website

betrayed him. He would accept no less than they be hanged from the same oak tree, and in return he promised he would trouble the King no more during his reign.

The keepers then prostrated themselves before the King and confessed their guilt. Despite their pleas for mercy, the furious King had them all hanged that night from Herne's Oak. Almost immediately, the deer began to return to the forest and Herne appeared no more during Richard's reign.

The day after the King's death in 1399, Herne's terrifying spectre rode back into the Great Park accompanied by a ghostly entourage of the executed traitors and a pack of hounds with flaming eyes forming his 'Wild Ride'. His presence has remained in Windsor Great Park ever since, appearing numerous times in a variety of forms over the centuries. The phenomena range from the sound of his hunting horn or the baying of his hounds, through to the full manifestation of Herne and his band of phantom hunters.

Sightings of Herne are said to be bad omens and usually foretell death or disaster for the individual who sees him, or the nation in general. It is said he appeared on the eve of Henry IV's death (1413), and several times during the reign of Henry VIII (1509-1547), when the bluff King Hal imposed his will at the expense of those around him. Legend has it that Henry himself saw him at the time of his marriage crisis with Anne Boleyn and Herne rose again before Charles I's execution in 1649.

During the twentieth century there was a spate of appearances at the time of momentous national events. A phantom white stag was seen in the forest just before the start of the First World War. Herne and his spectral band were seen just before the start of both World Wars (1914 and 1939), at the outset of the Great Depression (1931), just before the death of George V and Edward VIII's abdication (1936) and again before George VI's death (1952).

Count Nicolai Tolstoy in *The Quest for Merlin* relates a conversation he had with his old friend and poet Charles Richard Cammell, who was also at Eton before the Great War. He had spoken several times with an old keeper in the Park who had seen Herne plunge by on his ghostly chase.

Brigadier G.E.M. Baillie is reputed to have heard the huntsman's horn and the baying of hounds when a boy at Eton around 1910. He went on to win the Military Cross in the Great War and would have inherited the title of Lord Burton, head of the Bass brewing dynasty, had he not been killed in the Second World War.

One of the most documented 'sightings' of modern times came in October 1926 when a local magistrate Mrs Walter Legge heard the sound of Herne's hounds, twice in the space of a fortnight. After she had retired to bed for the night at her Old Windsor Farmhouse, which lay two fields distant from the boundary of Windsor Great Park, Mrs Legge was surprised to hear the sound of the baying of hounds. She recalled;

> *'It was exactly midnight, and I remember hearing the clock at Old Windsor striking the hour. The noise of the baying of the hounds was faint at first, increased in volume, and then died away in the direction of Windsor Castle.*
>
> *It was a very deep bay, like that of wolf hounds. Exactly two weeks later, again at midnight I heard the same thing. Directly afterwards my daughter, who had come from the floor above, knocked at my door and asked, "Did you hear that?"*
>
> *Not having spoken to my daughter of my first experience, I inquired, "Hear what?" Then she said, "They must have been Herne the Hunter's hounds."'*

It is known that the Prince of Wales (later King Edward VIII) referred to this incident during a Household Brigade Drag Hounds luncheon shortly afterwards. He had a keen interest in the paranormal and spent many a night ghost-hunting in Windsor Great Park.

In the spring of the following year further reports circulated of a phantom stag seen running in and out of the tree line either side of the Long Walk before disappearing in broad daylight.

The eighteenth century Royal Lodge was for over fifty years the home of Queen Elizabeth, the Queen Mother until her death in 2002. Today it is the home of Prince Andrew the Duke of York. However back in September 1947 shortly after the Royal Wedding of Elizabeth and Prince Philip, a spectral figure was reported near Royal Lodge where the newly-wed Royal couple were staying. A woman who lived in the Park said she was walking through the woods late at night when suddenly she saw the shadowy form of a horse and rider.

> *'The figure was 10 yards ahead of me. As I approached, he sensed my presence and uttering a maniacal laugh galloped off through the woods. Within a few seconds he vanished then I heard the sound of the hunting horn. I am not superstitious but I immediately thought that Herne was out riding again.'*

Eton schoolboys also seem to feature strongly in the sightings. In 1936, two Eton boys reported hearing the sound of hounds when walking near Herne's Oak and in 1962 two Eton schoolboys taking a late night short-cut through the forest apparently found an old hunting horn. Wondering how it would sound, one of the party blew it and within seconds encountered Herne thundering towards them riding a black horse accompanied by great hounds of a distinctive breed not seen in England for over five centuries. On this occasion the boys came to no harm but were terrified by the experience.

Similar stories have circulated around Windsor for many years. One concerns three lads who were playing truant in Windsor Great Park in the 1950s. One of them was a 'Teddy Boy', the name given to a stylish but rebellious juvenile delinquent of that time. The boys were making the most of their day off school by throwing stones, snapping branches off trees and similar anti-social behaviour.

As the boys wandered deeper into the forest, the 'Teddy Boy' noticed a curious old hunting horn hanging from a tree. He immediately went over and snatched it from the branch. His two companions knowing something about the legend of Herne the Hunter, told him to put it back and sensing something was amiss were anxious to leave the area. The 'Teddy Boy' in true defiant fashion blew it loudly in an act of bravado. Immediately something changed in the atmosphere and a deathly silence descended upon the area. All of a sudden they heard the sound of baying hounds and approaching horses crashing through the trees towards them.

The two local boys threw themselves to the ground in terror and covered their eyes, and told their companion to do the same. The sounds grew ever-closer and louder and in no time it seemed as though the deafening racket was upon them. It was all they could do to remain still, as the thundering hooves and snarls of great hounds passed over them.

One of the youths sneaked a look at his companion, whose eyes were screwed tightly shut, then glanced at the 'Teddy Boy' who was lifting his head to espy the source of the unholy commotion. He saw his eyes widen in panic as though his gaze had fallen upon something abominable. As he screamed in terror, the other boy reburied his face into the soil and curled tighter into a ball and prayed for protection. He heard the sound of a single arrow being loosed and striking a solid target and then the unearthly noises began to fade into the distance and almost immediately the sound of birdsong returned to the forest. The two boys slowly and with trepidation opened their eyes and looked about them. As they rose trembling to their feet, they realised their companion was no longer with them. Although they called out and searched the immediate area of the forest. He was nowhere to be found and he has never been seen since that day.

No records of missing 'Teddy Boys' or traumatised Eton schoolboys have emerged in recent years to my knowledge. The stories have all the hallmarks of an apocryphal tale told to keep young people on the straight and narrow. Having said that, should you encounter a hunting horn hanging from a tree whilst walking in Windsor Great Park, you would be well advised to keep on walking!

In 1931, Arnold Beckett, a regular visitor to the Great Park was walking through the forest contemplating heading back to the railway station to return home to London. He had become a little disorientated and had strayed into a clearing he was not familiar with. As he looked around him he was shocked to see a grotesque swinging corpse hanging from the lower limb of a great oak tree. Although his heart began racing, he ran towards the tree to cut the man down but stumbled in the long grass and fell flat on his face. When he looked up, the man and the tree had disappeared. Filled with an overwhelming feeling of dread he fled the forest. It was not until some time later that he confided in a friend, a Windsor schoolmaster, about the gruesome apparition. It was at this point that he first learnt of the legend of Herne the Hunter. Although intrigued by the story, Arnold Becket was sceptical that such sightings were bad omens. Six months later however, his business took a sudden turn for the worse and his life collapsed around him. His body was found hanging from a tree in Windsor Great Park.

Over the years many suicides by hanging have taken place in the Great Park. One with a specific reference to the ancient legend, dates back to the early 1970s. An investment banker, facing fraud charges left a suicide note claiming to have seen the ghost of Herne just before taking his own life. Another story reports a headless man seen around the enchanted tree and asserts it to be the ghost of a poacher who allegedly blew off his own head with a shotgun, after encountering the terrifying image of Herne whilst poaching in the moonlight.

Today Herne's Oak continues to attract tourists, Pagans and folklorists alike, fascinated by its long and unique history. However many do not realise, the current mighty oak is not the original, which was over 400 years old by the time Shakespeare immortalised it. The tree upon which Herne is said to have hanged himself was little more than a blasted stump by the end of the eighteenth century and sadly did not survive the reign of King George III. In 1796 when in the grip of his 'madness' and following an incident where he allegedly shook hands with a tree believing it to be the King of Prussia, George III mistakenly ordered the destruction of Herne's Oak. During a cull of 'aged and ugly' trees in the Great Park, the King sanctioned the clearance of several oaks which included Herne's. Courtiers were either unwilling or unable to countermand the order and the death warrant for Herne's Oak was signed. Later in a moment of lucidity, having been informed of the fate of the ancient tree, George was furious, initially denying responsibility for the decision, and then claiming that the 'true' Herne's Oak was in fact elsewhere. This deceived no-one, but Royal aides went along with the fiction when George anointed another mighty oak nearby, as the 'true' Herne's Oak.

This tree survived until the reign of Queen Victoria when it was blown down in gale on 31 August 1863 and logs from it were famously burned in her own fireplace in an attempt to *lay the ghost of Herne*. Wood from the fallen oak was also used to make several small pieces of furniture, among them a cabinet for the Queen, and a magnificent bust of William Shakespeare which once graced the Royal Library, and is currently in the possession of the Windsor Museum. Acorns were also gathered from the tree and sent across the empire for ceremonial plantings during Victoria's jubilee years in 1887 and 1897.

When King Edward VII ascended he throne in 1901 he was said to have disapproved of the siting of his mother's Herne's Oak and so in 1906 the fourth tree to bear the hallowed name was planted at the old chalk pit beside the 'faerie dell' where the original once stood.

There have been many unusual and unexplained sightings in Windsor Great Park over its long history but few have been as bizarre as the fabulous beast which appeared in broad daylight to an aristocratic lady early in the twentieth century.

In the early 1920s whilst walking alone through Windsor Great Park, on a bright summer morning, Sibell Lilias Blunt-Mackenzie, 3rd Countess of Cromartie (1878-1962), encountered a bizarre-looking animal slowly approaching her. It resembled an enormous hare and moved with a typical hare-like gait but was the size of a goat. As it came closer she saw it had a pair of curved horns and its face was half-goat, half-hare. The creature loped towards her without any fear. The countess was so astonished by this uncanny beast that she stood motionless as it passed by her. She told writer Violet Tweedale, that the creature passed by so close that she felt compelled to strike out at it with her parasol whereupon it vanished into thin air.

Although this may seem an unlikely and unfamiliar image to British eyes, in fact the legend of a horned hare exists in many cultures around the world. Between the sixteenth and eighteenth centuries the legendary horned rabbit, a hypothetical cross between the antelope and the hare appeared in several illustrations and accounts. The creature was even studied by several naturalists, who gave it the Latin scientific name *Lepus Cornutus*. In the USA the beast is referred to as a *Jackalope* and commonly features in folklore. The same animal is referred to in the forests of Bavaria as the *Wolpertinger*.

A phantom 'horned hare' was seen in Windsor Great Park by the Countess of Cromartie in the 1920s. Wikimedia Commons

Chapter 20
'BUTCHER' CUMBERLAND'S HAUNTED LODGE

CUMBERLAND LODGE IS a seventeenth century Grade II listed country house in Windsor Great Park. Although now occupied by a charitable educational foundation, it has a fascinating history and paranormal pedigree. It has been the home of several future Kings including George III and George IV and was a Royal residence until 1923. It was the site of secret negotiations leading up to the abdication of King Edward VIII and the film *The King's Speech* was made there.

The house was built in 1650 by John Byfield, a Captain in Cromwell's army. The house was called Byfield House until 1670 and then renamed New Lodge, and later Windsor Lodge.

After the Restoration, King Charles II renamed the house Ranger Lodge and made it the official residence of the Ranger of the Great Park – a Crown appointment always held by someone close to the sovereign and therefore a latter-day successor to Herne the Hunter.

John Churchill, 1st Duke of Marlborough, the hero of Blenheim died there in 1722, and it was his wife Sarah who had the title of Ranger bestowed upon her by Queen Anne. However it is not a Churchill ghost who haunts the Lodge, but one of its later Royal residents.

Cumberland Lodge's name is derived from the title of its first Royal inhabitant: Prince William, Duke of Cumberland, second son of George II who led the English massacre of the Scots at Culloden earning him the gruesome nickname of 'Butcher' Cumberland or 'Billy the Butcher'. He introduced a menagerie at the Lodge, and spent most of his retirement developing the house and landscaping the grounds.

His presence is said to be responsible for the icy cold spots and unsettling atmosphere which occasionally descends upon some parts of the house and his restless ghost has been blamed for a number of inexplicable incidents, most notably in the drawing room which was once the bedroom in which he took his last earthly breath.

During a recent harsh winter, a water pipe had burst in the kitchen necessitating the call-out of an emergency plumber who it transpired was also a psychic. Like many sensitives before him, as soon as he entered the house he could sense the presence of many spirits. The plumber mentioned his interest in the supernatural to the official who accompanied him around the house.

The official asked if he wanted to visit the drawing room as it was supposed to be the most haunted room in the Lodge.

The plumber eagerly accepted the offer and after he had carried out the repair in the kitchen they both set off towards the drawing room at the far end of the Fitzalan corridor. As they approached the door to the drawing room, the plumber was filled with a sense of foreboding and began to hesitate and express some reservations about going into the room. They crossed the Great Hall, rounded the main staircase, and arrived in the anteroom outside the drawing room.

The plumber was by now distinctly uneasy and said he felt very odd and preferred not to go in. The official reassured him and said that having come this far he might as well have a look. The guide slowly swung open the door and proceeded to enter the drawing room. As he stepped over the threshold, the plumber nervously followed behind. Just as he was entering the room the official flicked on the light switch, whereupon all the bulbs in the grand chandelier exploded at once causing the pair to flee down the corridor in terror. Whether it was a simple electrical malfunction, or the phantom of the Duke of Cumberland showing his disapproval of their intrusion into his bedchamber, remains unknown

A strange airborne omen occurred on the evening of 16 April, 1746 involving the father of the Duke of Cumberland, King George II. The King was walking on the terraces of Windsor Castle along with several courtiers, when suddenly he drew their attention to an unusual phenomenon in the sky.

In the clouds above Windsor the scene of a battle unfolded before their eyes. The figure of an armed Highlander was distinctly fighting with a British Grenadier. For several minutes the Grenadier appeared to be overpowered by the Highlander but eventually he rallied and the Highlander was beaten to his knees, his claymore was broken and his dirk was seen to fall from his hands. The Grenadier sealed his victory by stamping on his adversary and waving his arms in a gesture of triumph.

The curious clouds began to dissipate and the King called out *'Thank God! My Kingdom is saved.'* A fortnight later a messenger arrived at Windsor Castle bearing despatches from the Duke of Cumberland announcing that the Highlanders under The Young Pretender, Bonnie Prince Charlie, had been completely routed at Culloden on 16 April, the date that the cloud battle was witnessed by the English King and his entourage.

The revolting spectre of the bloated majesty of King George IV who died at Windsor Castle in 1820 is said to haunt both the Castle and Cumberland Lodge where he lived and held lavish parties during the Regency. If his restless spirit haunts the grounds it is hardly surprising. In death he was not allowed to rest in peace as Royal funeral attendants had to hurriedly drill a hole in the Royal coffin of the obese King, to release the build-up of putrefying post mortem gases, after an apparently botched embalming job.

George IV used Cumberland Lodge as a guest house to Royal Lodge during Ascot Week. He also diverted the road leading to the Castle (the Long Walk) at Snow Hill, where he erected a statue of his father known locally as 'The Copper Horse'. There have been several reports over the years of ghostly activity near 'The Copper Horse' and even armed Royal protection officers have reported feeling spooked when patrolling near the statue at night.

Soon after the statue was unveiled in 1830 a local legend grew that the sculptor had forgotten to put stirrups on the statue meaning the Royal rider would almost certainly have fallen off his mount. The statue was built in two parts and his omission only became apparent when it was put together, so the story goes. Overcome with shame, the sculptor hanged himself from the branch of an oak tree a short distance from his statue and his ghost has haunted the Long Walk ever since.

Sadly this is a purely fictional tale. The sculptor Sir Richard Westmacott had not *forgotten* the stirrups. George IV wanted the monument to his father to resemble the Romanesque statue of Peter the Great in St Petersburg and stirrups were not used by classical riders. Furthermore whatever is haunting Snow Hill is unlikely to be Sir Richard, who did not commit suicide there but lived to a ripe old age.

Snow Hill was however also the place where Henry VIII stood at the exact moment his second wife Anne Boleyn was facing her executioner at the Tower of London. Confirmation of her death was signalled by gunfire from the Round Tower and some have suggested it is the guilty ghost of Henry who haunts this place.

Chapter 21
THE FORGOTTEN GHOUL OF FROGMORE COTTAGE

FROGMORE HOUSE IS a palatial seventeenth-century house situated in the private part of the Park known as Home Park. It is renowned for its beautifully landscaped gardens in which Queen Victoria, at her own expense, built a mausoleum for her beloved Albert and where their bodies now lie together in eternal slumber.

Royal gardeners working in the Great Park have reported seeing phantom figures in the grounds around Frogmore House. On one occasion the figure of a 'grey man' was seen near the mausoleum which gardeners assumed was a visitor, before it disappeared in front of them. The former housekeeper of Frogmore House reported that several young girls who worked on the staff had seen fleeting figures within the mausoleum and were frightened to work there unaccompanied.

The most surprising account of the supernatural however emanates not from these grand buildings but the much more modest building which sits nearby. Frogmore Cottage nestling in the shadow of the magnificent royal residence of Frogmore House is an unlikely setting for a demonic sighting. However this was exactly what occurred at this historic abode in the heart of Windsor Great Park during the early part of Queen Victoria's reign.

This little known-story took place in the spring of 1844 when Henry James, the wealthy American theologian (and father of the novelist of the same name) rented Frogmore Cottage from the Duchess of Kent, Queen Victoria's mother, at what he described as *'an exorbitant rent'*, of £4.10s per week. He and his family intended to use the cottage as their home during their extended educational stay in England. By the end of that month however his life was to change forever after an encounter with a malevolent force in the house. Henry James's own description of what happened that fateful day is so vivid that it deserves to be quoted in full:

'… One day towards the close of May, having eaten a comfortable dinner, I remained sitting at the table after the family had dispersed, idly gazing at the embers in the grate, thinking of nothing, and feeling only the exhilaration incident to a good digestion, when suddenly – in a lightning flash as it were – fear came upon me, and trembling which made all my bones to shake.

To all appearance it was a perfectly insane and abject terror, without ostensible cause, and only to be accounted for, to my perplexed imagination, by some

damnèd shape squatting invisible to me within the precincts of the room, and
raying out from his fetid personality influences fatal to life.

The thing had not lasted ten seconds before I felt myself a wreck, that is reduced
from a state of firm vigorous, joyful manhood to one of almost helpless infancy.
The only self control I was capable of exerting was to keep my seat. I felt the
greatest desire to run incontinently to the foot of the stairs and shout for help to
my wife, to run to the roadside even, and appeal for the public to protect me; but
by an immense effort I controlled these frenzied impulses, and determined not to
budge from my chair till I had recovered my lost self-possession.'

This traumatic supernatural experience led to Henry James's breakdown
for many years. He later identified the phenomenon as that described by the
eighteenth-century philosopher Emmanuel Swedenborg as a state of spiritual
'*Devastation*' or '*Vastation*' or a total collapse of vital energies. Today we may
suggest it was a nervous breakdown but the suddenness of the incident
combined with James's otherwise sound mental and physical state at the time
of the ghoulish vision, indicates this may have been a classic case of 'demonic
possession'. Whatever it was, it led to a complete breakdown from which it
took him years to recover. Although all who knew him were aware that *some-*
thing had happened to Henry James during his time at Windsor, he kept the
precise details secret for over thirty-five years until he wrote his autobiography
in 1879 just three years before his death.

Interestingly Henry James's son Henry junior, the author of *The Turn of the*
Screw also lived in England for the latter part of his life, at Lamb House in Rye
in Sussex. He claimed he was frequently visited here by the ghost of an old
lady wearing a mantilla who inspired his gothic ghost stories. Perhaps he and
his father shared a psychic sensitivity. For one it became a muse for the other
a curse.

There have been many paranormal theories to explain what went on at Frogmore Cottage that spring. Herne's Oak lay just a short distance away and for
centuries a malevolent presence has been felt in the vicinity. A ley-line has also
been identified as running directly south from the foot of the Round Tower of
Windsor Castle, through several churches to an ancient roman building in
Surrey. This passes directly through the Great Park and may be responsible for
boosting latent paranormal forces in the area and could account for the prepon-
derance of supernatural activity observed around Windsor and the Great Park.
Indeed there are many who suggest that rather being a coincidence, it was the
very presence of ley-lines which encouraged our ancient forebears to build
earthworks, castles and sacred buildings where they did.

No other reports of the demonic being, which so affected Henry James
senior, at Frogmore Cottage have been discovered. Between the wars it became
home to exiled members of the Romanov dynasty who fled the Russian

revolution, including Prince Felix Youssoupov who, with others, killed 'The Mad Monk' Rasputin. More recently its colourful history has been all but forgotten and today it serves a much more mundane purpose as apartment accommodation for royal retainers.

PART FOUR
ETON

....

Chapter 22
ETON'S EERIE HIGH STREET

JUST A FEW paces from the battlements of Windsor Castle lies the historic town of Eton. Dominated by the stunning architecture of Eton College since 1440, this quiet town has been the focus of many awe-inspiring events. In 1537, escorted by the future 'Bloody' Mary as chief mourner, the funeral procession of Queen Jane Seymour passed down Eton High Street and rattled over the old wooden bridge before being taken into her tomb in St George's Chapel. So sudden had been Jane's death, that Eton authorities were forced to conduct hasty road repairs before the Royal procession arrived from Westminster.

Just a decade later, the body of Henry VIII was to pass down the same route on his journey to join the woman he married just eleven days after executing Anne Boleyn. History and bloodshed is never far away in Eton and it has a wealth of reported supernatural occurrences over the centuries. Indeed some of England's earliest ghost stories have their origins in these picturesque buildings.

With such a paranormal pedigree it was surprising therefore to discover the remarkable announcement posted in the London Times on 6 December 1904 advertising for a ghost to haunt Eton College. *(see overleaf)*

Was this simply a tongue-in cheek advertisement from Eton College or in fact a double-bluff response to fears emerging from the ruling classes that their privileged offspring would somehow be at risk from supernatural forces lurking in the dark recesses of these hallowed halls?

History shows there is no shortage of ghosts either in the town or at the college. The connections between Eton and the literary supernatural genre were also reinforced through the writings of one of the foremost authors of ghost stories, M.R. James, who was not only an Eton Old Boy but a former Provost of the College between the wars and who drew upon local legends in crafting his gothic tales of the supernatural.

In bygone centuries the ghost of the founder, Henry VI, was bizarrely believed to have taken the form of an enormous grey rat which haunted the cloisters and 'Royal rat-catching' became a great sport amongst the boys.

WANTED—A GHOST.

Painful Incompleteness of Old Eton College, England.

That famous English public school, Eton, wants a ghost. That is, of course, if the students and masters agree with the editor of the Eton College Chronicle, who sets forth the case as follows:

"The college is in itself a triumph of wasted space. It teems with forgotten rooms and superfluous box-rooms. If we are doomed to live in such an atmosphere, why cannot some enterprising person with a talent for organization give us a ghost?

"The vacancy by the school office would be haunted by some more than usually apocryphal victim of the barbarity of Keate—a boy who had died on being beaten fifteen times by mistake in the same morning, or some other unusual process. The recesses of the cloisters might be the hiding place of some hoard deposited by a mythical captain of the school who had poisoned all the college on Threepenny Day, with a skeleton of the same on top.

"The hole in the chapel wall would be the home of some badger or other contraband pet in days gone by; the same scenes would be haunted by choir boys assassinated by public subscription from an infuriated congregation.

"It would not be necessary to have actual spectres with chains, such as might be laid by a conduct and have their skeletons presented to the Eton College Museum. All we want is a really healthy basis of legend to lend associations of antiquity to the school in general, and strike unfeigned terror into the heart of the unsophisticated lower boy."

An advertisement in The Times, *6 December 1904.*

Another early but more conventional of Eton's hauntings is the 'Grey Lady'. A woman in medieval dress who is believed to be the ghost of Jane Shore, the charming and witty mistress of Edward IV who dissuaded the King from destroying the school in an act of spite against his Lancastrian rival Henry VI, who had established it. After the King's death she fell out of favour with the regime of Richard III and was accused of dabbling in the occult.

The trumped-up charges of sorcery and witchcraft could not be substantiated and the accusations against Jane Shore were reduced instead to being a harlot. The Bishop of London sentenced her to the traditional public penance for harlotry at St Paul's Cathedral. Jane in an unkempt state, dressed in only her petticoat, and draped with a white sheet, had to walk barefoot along the sharp flint stones of London. She carried a candle and walked in front of the cross and a choir singing psalms. Her accusers, expecting her to be jostled and jeered by the thronging crowd were astonished when, struck by her beauty and dignity, they were moved to pity her. Although this public humiliation backfired on her enemies, *'Jane Shore'* entered the vocabulary as popular rhyming slang for *whore* as suggested in this ditty republished in *The Ingoldsby Legends* in the early nineteenth century;

...While Louis Quatorze kept about him in scores,
What the Noblesse, in courtesy, term'd his 'Jane Shores',
They were called a much coarser name out of doors...

Following her public penance Jane Shore was incarcerated at the notorious Ludgate Prison for her crime. Her great beauty attracted the attention of the King's solicitor, Thomas Lynom, who entered into a contract of marriage with her whilst she was still a penniless prisoner. Petitioning by Lynom, supported by the Provost and Fellows of Eton College, who had been alerted to her plight, secured her release and resulted in a pardon from King Richard III.

Grateful Eton officials recalling her intervention to save the College granted her life-long lodgings in **Lupton's Tower** opposite the College Yard. Where it is said she died alone in 1527 at the age of eighty-two. Some accounts describe her living her final years in relative comfort whereas other reports suggest she was forced to beg in order to survive. Either way it seems that in death her spirit has continued to walk the earth as the 'Grey Lady of Eton' for almost 500 years.

In a well documented sighting in the more recent past, the deputy editor of the *Eton College Chronicle*, having worked late in compiling a forthcoming issue, was returning to his dormitory but decided against walking through the ancient cloisters and took a different route. As he entered a doorway leading onto Brewhouse Yard he saw a beam of light from Lupton's Tower illuminating a woman dressed in a long medieval gown. Initially he did not pay too much attention, but then noticed that although her legs appeared to be moving, she remained in the same position. At that point he became aware that he was witnessing paranormal activity and suddenly became uncontrollably frightened.

In panic, he fled as fast as his legs could carry him but avoiding his usual route which would have taken him through the graveyard. He describes what happened next:

'...I chose to go round by the Brewhouse Gallery. There was a board lying between Brewhouse Yard and School Yard. As I crossed it, it made its usual clumping sound. I walked hastily onwards. About five seconds later I heard the same clumping sound. The woman was following me. I ran towards Baldwin's Bec, my pulse beating fast. Before entering the door I looked round. I saw a sudden white flash and whatever had been following me disappeared.'

Perhaps Jane's troubled spirit continues to walk the cloisters of Eton, tormented by the injustices which were perpetrated upon her during her earthly life. Legend has it that her ghost walks the chambers of Eton College on Founder's Day the 4th of June. Some even claim to have seen the apparition gliding across the cobbled pavements carrying a candle as if reliving her penance.

The **Vice-Provost's Lodge** lies off the old cloister of the College and is associated with a number of ghosts. The first is believed to be the ghost of Dr John Keate, the famous headmaster who ruled the college with a rod of iron during the early nineteenth century. It was said of him that he had thrashed, in their schoolboy days, nearly all the men who became famous in the first half of the century. On one day, 30 June 1832, he beat 87 boys using 40 rods, replacing them as they broke and later regretted that he had not flogged them harder! In life, although diminutive in stature, he was an awe-inspiring figure to those he terrorised and possessed dark red hair and a fearsome booming voice 'like a fog horn'. According to Kinglake the historian, 'he wore a hat something between that of Napoleon Bonaparte and the head-dress of a widow woman.' The ghost of this awesome personage has never been seen, but for over a hundred years his ghostly footsteps have been heard to mount the heavy oak staircase leading from the quadrangle to the Upper School retracing his former route around the College in search of errant boys.

In a recent disclosure, horse racing pundit John McCririck reported that he had witnessed the ghost of an Eton school master on several occasions. McCririck, a pupil at the school in the 1950s, says he saw the ghostly figure of the master complete with gown and mortar board in the corridors at Eton each time he was about to be caned. Perhaps this crisis apparition was indeed the spectre of Dr Keate making his presence felt to ensure the deed was done to his satisfaction.

The resident ghost of a medieval boy at the Vice-Provost's Lodge is far less intimidating, indeed it tries its best not to disturb the living. Angus Macnaghten in *Haunted Berkshire* writes that between 1956 and 1959, Mr and Mrs Marsland occupied the second floor of the Vice-Provost's Lodge and much of it was used as storerooms by the College. One day Mrs Marsland heard the sound of someone coming quietly up the wooden staircase. She thought it was a particularly shy boy coming to get something signed, for each time she went out to see him he turned and took flight back down the staircase. After this had happened a number of times, it dawned on Mrs Marsland that her visitor was not flesh and blood.

Gradually she became used to hearing the boy approach and pretended to take no notice to see if he had the courage to come closer. Occasionally she became aware of him standing watching her at the kitchen doorway while she prepared the meals. Out of the corner of her eye she said he was about 5 feet 6 inches tall, dressed in a long dark grey medieval costume made of a coarse woollen material. She did not find it in the slightest frightening and enjoyed its company and said *'there was a very nice atmosphere whenever it was there.'* The figure visited at all times of the day but if ever she turned around to look at it, it simply vanished. She believed it to be the ghost of a college boy who died centuries before. In recent years the Vice-Provost has taken up residence once again in the Lodge and this shy spectre has not been seen there for some time.

Another ghost of a boy in medieval dress has also been seen haunting the meadows adjacent to the river at **Cuckoo Weir**. The apparition was seen by several people and widely reported in 1873 and has been seen on many occasions since. Eton College firmly believes in the 'The Spook of Cuckoo Weir' who is thought to have been a college boy who drowned in the Thames over four hundred years ago at a spot on the river just north of the school where Eton's swimming tests took place from 1529 well into the 1950s.

For many years the 'lower boys' bathed at a spot in the river which bore the ominous name of 'Dead Man's Hole' a name which later became incorporated into the *'Eton Fives'* ball game invented by Eton boys in 1877.

It was the archaic ritual to select a 'lower boy', bind his hands and feet together and throw him fully clothed into the deepest part of Cuckoo Weir whilst those watching timed the older boy whose turn it was to rescue him. It is believed that this hideous sport resulted in the death of one of the victims and the ghost of the drowned boy now haunts this section of the riverbank. The barbaric practice was also described by M.R. James in his classic *Collected Ghost Stories*.

The records show that many Eton boys drowned in the Thames over the centuries. By the mid nineteenth century it was estimated that one boy was drowned every three years until the Eton College authorities exercised greater supervision and control measures.

Eton Schoolboys swimming in the Thames at Cuckoo Weir. ©Wellcome Library London

Writer George Orwell was a pupil at Eton College. He was known to have a life-long fascination for the occult and a recent revelation in the biography of Orwell by Gordon Bowker suggests that he and another pupil were responsible for the death of a fellow Etonian through witchcraft.

Orwell was bullied when he arrived on a scholarship in 1917, by an older boy called Philip Yorke. Orwell was befriended by Steven Runciman who later went on to become a distinguished medieval historian, and the two schoolboys conspired to get their revenge using black magic and a wax effigy of the bully.

Orwell, whose real name was Eric Blair, had become interested in witchcraft after reading several volumes of ghost stories. These included *The Leech of Folkestone,* from *The Ingoldsby Legends*, about a maid skewering a wax image of her mistress in order to kill her.

Runciman later confessed in a letter written shortly before his death:

'Our making a wax effigy of an older boy whom we disliked for being unkind to his juniors was, I am ashamed to say, my idea . . . Blair found that interesting, and willingly collaborated. It was he who moulded the melted candle into a very crude human body.

He wanted to stick a pin into the heart of our image, but that frightened me, so we compromised by breaking off his right leg – and he did break his leg a few days later playing football – and he died young.'

The schoolboys were horrified when spell worked with such devastating effect. After breaking his leg their tormenter died within weeks of lymphatic leukaemia. This left Runciman racked with guilt and a terror of the supernatural. Orwell also spent the rest of his life convinced that he was responsible for Yorke's death and never spoke of it again, taking his secret with him to the grave in 1950.

A little further down the river lie the open meadows of Eton Wick leading to **Dorney Common**. In the dim and distant past this was waterlogged marshland and was known by travellers to have patches of treacherous bog. Local legend has it that a horse and carriage became trapped in the mud during a torrential storm centuries ago and disappeared into the marsh and was never found. On certain nights during thunderstorms, the ghostly apparition of the coach has been seen in the fields, its horse and rider struggling frantically to free themselves from the spectral quagmire before disappearing into the ground.

A shrouded figure has been seen on several occasions around the grounds and playing fields of Eton wearing a black cloak and a wide-brimmed hat described as looking like the man on the Sandeman's Port label. Two sisters who saw the figure walking towards them one evening in **Eton High Street** thought someone in fancy dress was approaching them until the figure turned into a doorway and disappeared. When they reached the doorway they found that it had been bricked up and there was no sign of the ghostly cloaked figure.

Several of the old houses along the Slough Road have reported supernatural activity over the years. A regular haunting took place at Coleridge House in **Keate's Lane**. One of the rooms at the back of the house was used as a spare room from which sounds were frequently heard of someone moving about inside and the opening and shutting of drawers. This occurred on several occasions. The housemaster's wife Mrs Hubert Hartley used to sleep in the next room and when this happened she described a 'miasma' or supernatural mist coming through the wall. She would go to the room and listen at the door to the noises going on within, then swiftly open the door in order to confront the perpetrator. Each time the noises stopped instantly – and the room was found to be quite empty.

During the 1920s the sons of Lady (Nancy) Astor, who lived at the magnificent Cliveden House along the River Thames at Taplow, were lodged at Coleridge House. Although they never saw or heard any paranormal activity themselves, they were well aware of others that had, and reported it to their mother who had a keen interest in the supernatural. It is rumoured that in order to safeguard the welfare of her boys she arranged for a secret exorcism service to be carried out there. Sources close to the family however suggest that as she was a committed Christian Scientist, she was unlikely to elicit the services of a priest. Whether or not the noisy presence remains is uncertain as the old house was demolished several years ago to create an extension for another boys' boarding house. The haunting has not been reported again … yet.

Ghost photographs are extremely rare but two are associated with the College. One was taken in the mid 1950s by the late Mr C. R. N. Routh an Eton Master since 1920 and a keen amateur photographer. Whilst taking photographs for the College archives inside the magnificent fifteenth-century **College Chapel**, he took a photo from the organ loft of the altar and the old east window. When it was developed he could see two shadowy figures in the print. Once enlarged he could see it was an elderly couple gazing at the altar with their backs to the camera. The old man was leaning on a gnarled stick and his wife had a slight stoop. Mr Routh was convinced that no-one came in or out of the Chapel while he was there and that his camera had captured the spirits of two long-departed visitors to the Chapel. The current whereabouts of this picture is unknown.

The second incident took place nearby at **Tangier Island** which nestles between the College Chapel and the River Thames. The island is home to the beautiful Luxmoore Garden where the ghostly image of its creator was captured on film in the late 1920s.

H.E. Luxmoore (1841-1926) was a well-respected Eton Housemaster and life-long friend of his former pupil M.R. James. He was passionate about gardening and created a garden on Tangier Island beside the Chapel in which he used to spend most of his leisure time. After his death at the age of eighty-six his friends erected a pavilion in his honour and commissioned a photograph to commemorate his forty-four years loyal service to the College at the ceremony of dedication. A photograph was taken of the dais, on which the official group stood facing the pavilion, with their backs to the camera. When it was developed the unmistakeable figure of the late Mr Luxmoore with flowing white hair could be seen standing amongst the guests with his stick, hunched shoulders and trademark short cape. The photograph was exhibited in Kissack's the photographer's window at 130 High Street for many years and those who saw it were in no doubt that it was the image of the well-known Eton Master captured after his death.

A fascinating story from Eton during the blackout at the height of the Secord World War also took place on Tangier Island at the waterworks.

It was the habit of the night shift workers to take a tea break at midnight when the local police Sergeant would cycle down the lane to join them for a cuppa and catch up on the latest gossip. Although the external walls had been sandbagged to protect the waterworks from a bomb blast, the workers could still hear the tick-tick-ticking of the free wheel of his bike as the policeman approached and would take this as their cue to put the kettle on.

One night the workers heard the familiar sound of the approaching cycle followed as usual by sound of the Sergeant's footsteps on the gravel walking towards them. They put the kettle on but were surprised when he never actually entered the mess room. They assumed he had been called away and thought nothing more of it. The following night however, the very same thing happened again. They heard the approach of the bicycle followed by the steady footsteps walking towards the mess room door, and waited in anticipation for the policeman to enter but the door never opened. The workers looked at each other with a mixture of apprehension and fear until one of them plucked up the courage to open the door and look outside. The door slowly creaked open but there was nothing there. No sign of a bike or the bobby. They settled their nerves with a cup of strong sweet tea and regained their composure before going back to work. Still somewhat unsettled by the night's events, they mentioned it to the early shift that relieved them the following morning. *'Oh hadn't you heard?'* came the reply, *'The old Sergeant died a couple of nights ago.'*

To this day people have reported hearing the tick-tick-ticking of the old Sergeant's bike as it continues its phantom night patrol around the town but as yet no-one has reported coming face to face with the ghostly policeman.

Most of the hostelries in Eton date back centuries and several have documented supernatural and poltergeist activity. One of the earliest ghost stories in England involves a ghost seen at an Eton inn back in the reign of Charles II.

The **Christopher Inn** was built in 1511 and originally stood on Baldwin's Bridge near the top of the High Street, next to the college. By the mid nineteenth century it had established an 'improper' reputation and was such a source of distraction for the elder boys who were attracted by the liquor and loose women, that the Master of Eton College, Dr Hawtrey, described it in 1845 as:

'... The cause of much evil and temptation among the boys.'

Taking the opportunity to acquire the building from the Crown, the Eton Authorities had the inn closed down and converted into College lodgings. A 'new' Christopher Inn however reopened some time later at its current location in the High Street, further away from the College, where to this day it remains a popular local hostelry.

However 350 years ago, the Christopher Inn it was the scene of a mesmerizing and long-forgotten ghostly encounter. This account was first brought to the attention of the world by Joseph Glanvil in his 1681 treatise on witchcraft, *Sadducismus Triumphatus*. It later received wider circulation in *Satan's Invisible World Discovered* published in 1769 and the story has remained unaltered over the centuries.

Captain William Dyke and Major George Sydenham were friends and military colleagues and had a keen interest in the after-life. One evening in Dulverton, Somerset, after a heated discussion on the immortality of the soul, they agreed a solemn promise;

'... that he who should die first on the third night after his funeral, between the hours of twelve and one, come to the little house which is here in the garden, and there give a full account to the survivor, who should be sure to be present there at the set time ...'

Major Sydenham was the first of the two to die and Captain Dyke held the midnight vigil as promised, but nothing happened. Dyke continued on with his life and thought no more about it. About six weeks later he travelled to Eton with his son who had been accepted there as a pupil. Travelling with them was his cousin Dr Thomas Dyke. They stayed at the Christopher Inn for three nights but on the final morning the Doctor was surprised not to find his cousin at breakfast. When he did appear he was in a state of complete nervous shock. The Doctor, seeing him shaking and trembling with hair on end and eyes staring wildly, asked what was the matter. Captain Dyke replied: *'I have seen the Major.'*

The Doctor thought he was joking but seeing the tormented demeanour of his cousin, realised he was serious. The Captain solemnly asserted, *'If ever I saw him in my life, I saw him but now,'* and then related to the Doctor what had taken place.

'This morning, after it was light, someone came to my bedside and suddenly drawing back the curtains, called, "Cap! Cap!"'

Struggling to maintain his composure, Dyke explained that he looked up in bright daylight to see the unmistakeable figure of his dead comrade looming over his bed and calling out the nickname which was so familiar to him.

Rigid with fear the Captain stuttered *'What, Major?'* To which the alarming apparition returned:

'I could not come at the time appointed, but I am now come to tell you, That there is a God, and a very just and terrible one, and if you do not turn over a new leaf you shall find it so.'

The Captain watched as the phantom approached a table on which sat a sword which had been given to him by the Major. The ghost walked mournfully around the timbered bedchamber and then snatched up the sword and drew it from its scabbard and thrust the rusty blade towards his fear-stricken friend saying:

'Cap! Cap! This sword did not used to be kept after this manner, when it was mine.'

This curious and cryptic portent of doom had a significant effect on Captain Dyke who never recovered from this harrowing spiritual encounter. He was plunged into a rapid physical and mental decline and his previous happy-go-lucky demeanour became *'strangely altered ... and he was unable to eat much.'* He was unable to shake off the profound effect that the nocturnal visitation had upon him and within two years he followed his old friend to the grave and the Christopher Inn at Eton forever became linked with the mysterious death of Captain Dyke.

The **Henry VI** pub (previously The Boaters and The Three Tuns) at 37 High Street can lay claim to being one of Eton's most haunted pubs. Vic Strangewick and his wife who ran the pub in the 1970s reported several occasions of being pushed by an unseen hand whilst working in the bar. The subsequent landlord Bert Matthews a former policeman and professional boxer, was more sceptical until he personally experienced the same phenomenon, and his wife saw the door handle to the empty upstairs quarters turn by itself. In 1979 a female customer saw the ghost of a man standing behind the landlord at a point behind the bar where an old wall had been knocked down.

Customers reported having their drinks poured over them by the mischievous spirit which haunts the pub but actual sightings have been few and far between. The only reported apparition was witnessed by the cleaner Mrs. Metcalfe who was unaware of any previous history when she the ghost of a man *'in quite modern clothes'* standing at the 'little middle bar' early one morning. As she looked towards it, the phantom figure slowly faded away. The resident ghost appears to have behaved himself of late, as the current owner reports no recent mischief.

Perhaps the Henry VI ghost has changed his 'regular' as a very similar apparition has been seen at another pub just down the road at 77 High Street. The 300-year-old **Prince George Inn** (formerly The Hogshead and The George) is also haunted by an elderly man who has been seen sitting at a table in the corner of the bar before slowly disappearing. The only clue to his identity came a few years ago when Mia, a new member of staff, was approached by an old lady and asked *'Have you seen my husband dearie?'* When Mia jokingly asked where she had left him, the old lady replied *'Oh no dearie … He's been dead for years but he haunts this place and I wondered whether you'd seen him yet!'*

Mia confessed she was rather unsettled by this ghostly revelation and although she never saw the phantom figure herself, it explained why several of the bar-staff complained of an uncomfortable atmosphere on occasions and did not like to be alone in the pub in the evenings. Mia became so apprehensive of an inevitable encounter with the old gent, that she left the pub not long after his wife's visit.

At 84-85 High Street is the **Crown and Cushion** pub. This has been an inn since 1753, although the building dates back to 1600. The pub is known locally to be haunted, but those who live and work in the premises are reluctant to talk about their supernatural experiences. Early one evening PC Mike Selby and his crewmate were driving down Eton High Street when a terrified young woman flew out through the doors of the Crown and Cushion into the road ahead of them. PC Selby stamped on the brakes and could tell straight away from her demeanour that something was seriously wrong. Fearing there was a troublemaker in the pub; the officers jumped out of the car and asked what was going on.

The young woman turned out to be the barmaid and after a little coaxing, explained that she had been changing the barrels when she had been terrified by an *'awful presence down in the cellar'* and just had to get out of the place. The bemused officers looked at each other with trepidation, and tentatively asked if there was anything they could do. Much to their relief, the young woman, who had by now regained her composure, declined their offer telling them that it was always happening and it was just something she had to put up with! The officers chose not to investigate further as they conveniently had to 'respond to an emergency call' and drove off at high speed. To this day we do not know what petrified the plucky young barmaid that evening, or what entity lurks still in the cellar.

The **Waterman's Arms** in Brocas Street has been a pub since 1844 but the building dates back several centuries. Lying close to the River Thames at the Brocas at Eton, it takes its name from its long association with the boatmen who punted passengers across the river to Windsor for a few pennies. In the mid 1980s, the new licensee of the Waterman's Arms reported that he had experienced some strange activity since taking over the pub. Optics had been drained and glasses moved. Initially he had suspected light-fingered bar staff, but having marked the labels one night, he found that by morning several had been drained even though there was no-one else on the premises. This remained unexplained and over the months he experienced further supernatural activity including strange bangs in the night, the sound of the pint pots hanging over the bar clinking together and a knocking noise coming from the walls of the pub.

He later discovered that previous landlords had also reported hearing odd noises in the pub going back centuries including miserable sounds of groaning and sighing coming from the ancient dank cellar. One explanation that has been suggested for these phenomena is that during the Great Plague of 1665 Windsor and Eton was ravaged with disease and the cellar of the pub was used as a makeshift mortuary to store the bodies of the victims as they were brought up the Thames on boats. Perhaps the restless spirits of the bubonic plague victims still haunt this historic pub?

Many years ago the ghost of a small sad boy with long hair, dressed in rags was clearly seen in the bar before suddenly disappearing. On another occasion the phantom ragamuffin was seen warming his hands by the fire. One of the previous incarnations of the pub was as the parish workhouse from 1792. Was the little ragged boy one of the pitiful souls who lived and died there?

The Waterman's Arms is also unique in claiming two famous Old Etonian highwaymen as ghosts in residence. One is Henry Simms who because of his flamboyant dress, educated demeanour and trademark large cutlass became known amongst the criminal underworld, as 'Gentleman Harry'. In fact Simms did not attend Eton but was an orphan from St Martin-in-the-Fields who, despite having academic potential, went into a life of crime from the age of ten by shoplifting and pick-pocketing. Despite being chained to the kitchen sink for a month by his grand-mother to prevent him re-offending, Simms used his charisma, time and again to con and rob the old lady. His fascinating life of highway robbery, transportation, escape and more robberies was captured in his own biography written in Newgate Prison whilst awaiting execution. In Newgate he fell in love with Mary Allen who was also on death row for stealing. After a short but intense prison romance, the couple who became known as 'The Gallows Lovers' were hanged together at Tyburn, whilst holding hands on 17 June 1747. Why he should haunt the Waterman's Arms is a mystery. He is however believed to have used the famous inn as a watering hole whilst on his nefarious activities.

William Parsons was an equally colourful figure and back in the late eighteenth century became notorious as the gentleman highwayman who never wore a mask. He was the son of Sir William Parsons and did attend Eton College for nine years most of which he spent gambling and swindling at the Christopher Inn and the Waterman's Arms.

His criminal career began with shoplifting a copy of Pope's *Homer* from an Eton High Street bookshop. The beating he received as punishment did nothing to deter him from developing into a thorough scoundrel, much to the chagrin of his despondent father who had him enlisted into the navy. Parsons however twice jumped ship and returned to England to continue his spree of fraud, debauchery and highway robbery. After a string of swindles, he was arrested and it was only the intervention of his influential father who saved him from the gallows. Parsons was sentenced to seven years transportation to the Colonies. After arriving in Maryland, he was befriended by a gentleman who fell for his sob-story of falling on hard times, and had him freed from his fetters. He repaid him by stealing his horse, guns and valuables and galloped back to the docks committing a string of highway robberies which paid his passage back to London.

Gambling and loose women ensured his ill-gotten gains did not last long and he was soon back in the saddle as a highwayman, which he often carried out with great charm. He once returned a wedding ring to a female victim and shook the hand of her husband. His luck however ran out at Windsor when, whilst lying in wait for a victim, he was recognised by Mr Fuller who had prosecuted him prior to his transportation. He was apprehended and taken to The Rose and Crown at Hounslow where he surrendered his weapons and pleaded for mercy. He had just persuaded his captors to release him, when they were joined by the landlord who recognised him as the highwayman who had plagued the area for weeks. He was tried for the crime of returning from transportation and despite pleas for clemency from his father, he was sentenced to death. On 11 February 1751 at the age of thirty-four, the gentleman highwayman was hanged in front of a baying crowd at Tyburn, perhaps regretting his trademark modus operandi of never wearing a mask.

Even today the current owners of the Waterman's Arms report an 'atmosphere' in some of the rooms. One of the bedrooms facing the Thames, in particular, possesses an icy chill all year round no matter what the weather. Despite having installed a huge radiator, the room defies all attempts to heat it and residents often believe it is being permanently cooled by air-conditioning.

An even more chilling supernatural episode took place at the end of the High Street at **The House on the Bridge,** now called *Côte Brasserie* which is a beautifully situated historic restaurant. Nestling on the banks of the Thames with the Castle creating a stunning backdrop, it welcomes tourists, locals and Old Etonians alike to partake of its fine cuisine and elegant traditional English ambiance. Al fresco diners who lazily contemplate the flotilla of pleasure craft passing beneath the terraced verandas could scarcely imagine that they are sitting at the scene of a terrifying haunting which left one family scarred with memories which they continue to relive to this day.

Back in the mid 1970s Helen Green's father owned The House on the Bridge. Helen had recently married Steve and was pregnant with their first child.

Helen explained: *'Steve had taken on the role of manager at the restaurant. The property had been neglected for a few years and was in need of refurbishment. We were cash-strapped at the time and decided to move into the property to save on rent. We couldn't believe our good fortune in living in a house with one of the best views in England.'*

Their excitement was however short-lived. One night shortly after moving in, Helen and Steve were asleep in the bedroom when they were awoken by a loud bang coming from the room next door. They knew the room was unoccupied and empty apart from a few removal boxes. Their initial curiosity quickly turned to fear when before they could get out of bed, the banging noises starting getting louder and louder like heavy furniture being dragged across a wooden floor.

Helen recalled: *'We were absolutely rigid with terror as the banging and crashing noises coming from next door filled the room. It sounded like someone crazed turning over furniture yet we knew there was nothing like that in the room.'*

Then a blood curdling scream rang out in the night, followed by the sound of a violent struggle like someone fighting for their life against an attacker. Paralysed with sheer terror, the couple huddled together in bed whilst the unholy sounds from the adjacent room continued unabated.

'We clung to each other under the bedclothes for what seemed like an eternity praying for daylight to come. We thought the nightmare would never end. We have never been so petrified in all our lives.'

As dawn broke the sounds finally subsided and as daylight streamed in through the curtains Steve and Helen, still shaken from their ordeal, got out of bed and tiptoed towards their bedroom door. They fled outside into the street, still in their nightclothes, their hearts racing after their night of fear. Once they had caught their breath they summoned up the courage to approach the room from where the supernatural sounds had emanated. They slowly opened the door half fearing what would await them on the other side. As they entered they were both astonished and relieved to find the room exactly as they had left it. The half a dozen or so cardboard boxes were still in place. There was nothing heavy in the room to have accounted for the unearthly banging and dragging noises which they both heard throughout the night. There was no upturned furniture, no blood on the walls and no gruesome cadavers on the floor in the way they had imagined in their minds eye – nothing at all in fact out of the ordinary.

Yet they had both heard an infernal struggle taking place just the other side of their bedroom wall which lasted for much of the night. Steve and Helen were bewildered and remain so to this day. There was no doubt that their experience was real. They both describe the incident as the most frightening night of their lives. Helen's father stayed with them the following night but there was no re-occurrence of this paranormal activity and never has been since. The source of the phenomenon remains a mystery but it seems what Helen and Steve witnessed that night was a psychic replay of a violent and bloody incident which had taken place back in the mists of time. Parapsychologists believe this phenomenon to be a 'psychic recording' in which traumatic incidents of high emotion and suffering are captured in the ether and replayed during certain circumstances.

Such instances are extremely rare. Many believe that these incidents are constantly being replayed in another dimension but are invisible to most of us, and can only be perceived by those sensitive enough to receive the signal or during periods when environmental and psychic conditions are in harmony such as the anniversary of a particular event. Were Helen and Steve especially attuned to such phenomena or was there something special about that particular night?

Although there is no firm documentary evidence, local legend talks of a murder taking place on the banks of the River Thames at the exact place where The House on the Bridge now stands. Although details have been lost over the passage of time, a young boy was murdered in what was described as a cowshed adjoining the building, which is now the restaurant. We do not know the motivation for the killing or whether the perpetrator was ever caught but perhaps what Helen and Steve witnessed that night was the anguished spirit of that murdered boy re-living his violent and tragic death as he wanders eternity seeking justice.

A strange phenomenon was reported by a delivery driver which occurred just before Christmas in 2002, although the precise location has not been confirmed. Just after dusk at around 7.30pm he was travelling from Eton towards Windsor when he turned into what he described as, *'a dark road completely free of traffic.'* He was at once gripped by an overwhelming fear, the like of which he had never before experienced. The sudden and inexplicable feeling of dread got worse and worse until it became absolute terror. It was only when the driver came to a roundabout and turned off that the fear began to recede and he regained his composure. The source of this acute sensation of fear has never been identified. Perhaps he passed through an area of high paranormal energy associated with one of Eton's many hauntings.

The Old Cockpit Inn, Eton High Street.
Wikimedia Commons

Back along the High Street stands the former **Old Cockpit Inn**, the oldest building in the High Street which dates back to the fifteenth century. Locals colourfully claim that Charles II used to travel down to this pub in disguise to wager on cockfights, although this is unlikely as it is now believed that the medieval 'cockpit', after which the inn was named, was in fact an abattoir.

Its ghostly resident is a small busy woman who has been seen from time to time as a 'Grey Lady' flitting between tables and trying to be as unobtrusive as a ghost can be. She is believed to be the phantom of a servant or waitress who lived and worked there during the long history of the inn. Her presence is considered to be benign and successive owners have had no difficulty in co-habitating with her. At the time of writing, this wonderful old building stands empty awaiting a new owner and consequently the 'Grey Lady' has not been evident of late.

Directly opposite the Old Cockpit is **97 High Street** which has long been the home of the ghost of Anne Hester who is never seen but often heard. The three storey house dates back to the early seventeenth century. Miss Hester was born there in 1857 and lived with her father, a prosperous master grocer, and her brother and sister. She never married and died there at the age of eighty in 1937. She had been a large woman and can still be heard walking rather heavyfootedly upstairs, and particularly in her own bedroom where she spent most of the latter part of her life.

During the 1940s it was later the home of theatre impresario Jack Minster and his wife Barbara Cochran-Carr who enjoyed sharing the house with Miss Hester for many years, although many of their guests refused to enter her haunted bedroom, the door to which could never be kept closed. Guests reported being barged out of the way on the stairs by the bulky form of Miss Hester. The sounds of doors slamming and heavy footsteps up and down stairs, accompanied by the rustling of her skirt, are amongst the other noisy phenomena experienced in this haunted Georgian house.

Number **51 High Street** is an impressive timbered Tudor building dating back many centuries. More recently it was an antiques shop owned by Charles Toller who lived above the shop with his family. It was haunted by a friendly ghost who again was never seen but often sensed by the family pets. Often the dog would get up and wag his tail to welcome the unseen visitor while the cat would rub against invisible legs. The most unusual occurrence was the ghostly appearance of an inanimate object. One day their fifteen-year-old son returned home from boarding school and went upstairs to fetch a book from the drawing room. On coming downstairs he noticed his parents had acquired a new piece of furniture. He asked his mother when she had bought the coffer or dough bin under the window. His mother knew that there was only a tripod table under the window and suggested he had made a mistake and needed to look again which he did, only to find the coffer had disappeared. Was this a simple mistake on the part of the young man or was this an example of a 'time slip' in which we are given a glimpse of life as it was decades or centuries before?

Further down the High Street in a sitting room above another antique shop, a family was scared stiff when they saw the ghost of a woman walk in front of them. Even more shocking was the fact that she was levitating 18 inches above the floor. It was not until the premises was inspected by Eton College surveyors, who own the property, that they realised that the floor had been lowered many years before.

The family learnt that this apparition was the latest of many unsettling incidents. The previous tenant had been an antique dealer who was knocked down and killed by a car outside the shop. He bequeathed the contents of the house to his staff who took away what they wanted but left behind several items which were still there when the new tenants moved in. The family were immediately struck by the unwelcoming atmosphere in the house and they were disturbed constantly at night by the sound of heavy footsteps on the stairs. The mother-in-law of the new tenant came to stay and at once complained about the disturbances, and put it down to the 'old fashioned' furniture and bric-a-brac which had been left in the shop. She insisted that all the reminders of the old tenant should be destroyed. The family removed and burnt furniture, clothing, pictures and many other objects.

The nightly procession of footsteps stopped, but one night the family was awoken in bed by screams coming from their nine-year-old daughter's bedroom. They all rushed to the room in a state of panic and were confronted with a terrifying shapeless entity which they could not describe but which was throwing itself all around the room. They snatched the little girl from the room and slammed the door shut, but the alarming commotion continued inside for several minutes. They did not dare open the door again that night, but the next morning they found the bedclothes had been torn and objects strewn all around the bedroom. This appeared to be the final angry act of a troubled spirit who reacted violently to their possessions being destroyed. There was no further recurrence but the bedroom remained unoccupied and unused for many years.

Thomas' Hairdressers at 19 High Street is a wonderful old Victorian barber-shop still fitted out with period fittings from the golden age of facial hair when gentlemen sporting bristling handlebar moustaches and mutton chop side-boards, were attended to by old fashioned barbers wielding cut-throat razors.

Back in the 1880s Henry Jefferies ran a fancy goods shop at the premises which was purchased by Frederick Betteridge who ran it as a popular hair-dressers. His son tragically committed suicide by cutting his throat with an open razor in the shop after a fit of depression. Staff who now work there believe he is the restless spirit who has never left the premises and who is responsible for objects being mysteriously moved and the cold spots which customers still experience when enjoying a haircut or a cup of coffee. Scissors and hairdressing tools are regularly moved up to 15 yards from where they should be, and the current owner reports his dog refuses the enter the premises at night.

Further along the western side lies number **117a High Street** which for many years was the home and surgery of Doctor Richard W.L. May. He was a popular and respected physician and known for his kind ways with children. After his death in the 1960s his friendly ghost began to haunt his former home and the children of successive generations of tenants have seen the apparition of a *'little old man in brown'* and have not at all been troubled by his genial ghostly appearances. Others have seen him complete with trilby hat visiting the houses of former patients in the High Street.

Chapter 23
THE DEMONIC CHURCH OF
ST JOHN THE EVANGELIST

JUST NEXT DOOR to this house, down a tree-lined path, lies the Victorian parish church of St John the Evangelist which holds a dark and deeply disturbing secret.

Tourists marvelling at its gothic splendour would never imagine that St John the Evangelist is believed by some to hold the unenviable distinction of being the only House of God forced to close by the actions of the Devil.

Patronised by Queen Victoria and Prince Albert who laid the foundation stone in 1852, this beautiful example of Victorian church architecture, once boasted over 1000 worshippers. However in 1981 parishioners fled its pews in droves when the church was plunged into the centre of a religious maelstrom after stories appeared in the Sunday tabloids about it being possessed by demons.

In a storyline more reminiscent of a Hammer horror film, reports emerged about unholy activities going on at the church. Windows were unaccountably smashed and candles found mysteriously lit around the altar as if in preparation of a satanic mass.

Religious artefacts were strewn around the building and an evil presence descended upon the church. Amidst wild speculation and sensationalised reporting, came confirmation in an astonishing statement from the parish vicar Reverend Christopher Johnson that he had been battling for months with the occult forces of evil who had taken over his church. Rev. Johnson who had been the vicar of St John the Evangelist since 1968 was quickly gagged by Church authorities, anxious to keep the matter under wraps. His wife Mrs Anne Johnson however was more defiant and verified that the couple had been living in terror, after being subjected to psychological and physical attack from the entity. She told the press:

'I have felt physical pain. I have been frightened. It may sound irrational but there are forces here to be reckoned with. Everyone is convinced that the mysterious incidents at the church are the result of evil spirits, not vandals.'

In addition to the desecration of religious relics, church vestments had been spirited away and the screams and shrieks of young girls had been heard echoing around the church walls. It was reported that the Rev. Johnson had awoken one night in terror being throttled by invisible hands. It was at this point that he took the unprecedented step of calling in the diocesan exorcist. Rev. Anthony Duncan who conducted the exorcism said afterwards;

'There certainly was an evil presence when I did the cleansing ceremony. It was one of the most unpleasant I've ever done.'

Although the malign presence was weakened for a while by the exorcism, within a short time it returned with a vengeance and became stronger and more destructive than ever, gaining such a grip over the church that only a handful of determined worshippers remained to support the beleaguered Reverend and Mrs Johnson. In desperation she told the press:

'There is evil here. It has driven people from the church. It is real and it is frightening.'

After all efforts to rid the church of the demonic spirit failed, Church authorities reluctantly took the extraordinary decision to close the church and re-locate the Reverend and Mrs Johnson.

The full details of this terrifying haunting and the torment caused to Rev. Johnson and his wife have never been disclosed. Even today locals refuse to talk about the evil that appeared in their midst. Church officials also remain tight-lipped about exactly what went on, and the official explanation for the closure was cited as 'falling congregations and rising maintenance costs.'

Why the sudden evil descended on the quiet parish church in Eton, subjecting a vicar and his wife to an ordeal of terror and anguish, remains a mystery. In the early 1980s there were a number of outlandish theories circulating, including one which claimed the church had been built on an ancient pagan site and that human sacrifice and devil worship had taken place there. It is known that early Christianity attempted to obliterate the influence of paganism by building on top of their sacred sites and there has indeed been a Christian church at that location since at least the fifteenth century, but there is no evidence to support the ancient pagan theory which appears to be little more than wild conjecture.

The church sat neglected and abandoned for almost a decade. The local beat officer had to contend with a string of break-ins and vandalism perpetrated by would-be Satanists eager to desecrate the church with their diabolical ceremonies. In order to bring an end to the disorder, demolition was seriously mooted by the Church authorities. However Eton College stepped in and purchased the church in 1991, saving it from the wrecking ball, once again returning it to a community resource. Today it houses the College sanatorium, together with staff accommodation and the lower part of the chancel serves as the town medical centre and doctors' surgery.

This disturbing case does however end on a positive note. In a quiet private ceremony on 13 September 1991, the Bishop of Buckingham, the Right

Reverend Simon Burrows re-consecrated a small chapel on the upper floor for public worship and this is occasionally used for services today. By this gesture the church has been snatched back from the clutches of the Devil and good has hopefully triumphed over evil, fulfilling the prophetic last public statement made by the Reverend and Mrs Johnson a decade previously:

'This is not the end of the story. We will not give up. The evil that is here will be driven out.'

St John the Evangelist church, Eton before the removal of the steeple and invasion by demons.
Wikimedia Commons

BIBLIOGRAPHY

BARHAM, Tony, *Witchcraft in the Thames Valley*, Spurbooks Limited, Bucks 2006

LONG, Roger, *Haunted Berkshire*, The History Press, Gloucestershire 2011

MACKLIN, John, *World's Most Bone-Chilling True Ghost Stories*, Sterling Publishing, New York 1993

MACNAGHTEN, Angus, *Windsor Ghosts and Other Berkshire Hauntings*, Countryside Books, Newbury 1976

MACNAGHTEN, Angus, *Haunted Berkshire*, Countryside Books, Newbury 1986

McLOUGHLIN, Ian, *Ghosts of Berkshire*, Countryside Books, Newbury 1995

MORSHEAD, Sir Owen Frederick, *Windsor Castle*, Phaidon Press, London 1957

RICE, Hilary Stainer, *Ghosts of the Chilterns and Thames Valley*, Corinthian Publishers, Slough 1986

SERGEANT, Philip W., *Historic British Ghosts*, Hutchinson and Co., London 1936

WILSON, Colin, *Mysteries*, Watkins Publishing, London 2006